The
COUNTERFEITERS
—— OF ——
BOSQUE REDONDO

The COUNTERFEITERS OF BOSQUE REDONDO

SLAVERY, SILVER AND THE U.S. WAR AGAINST THE NAVAJO NATION

MATT FITZSIMONS

FOREWORD BY LYNDA TELLER PETE

THE History PRESS

Published by The History Press
Charleston, SC
www.historypress.com

Copyright © 2022 by Matt Fitzsimons
All rights reserved

Cover image by William J. Carpenter. *Library of Congress*.

First published 2022

Manufactured in the United States

ISBN 9781467151429

Library of Congress Control Number: 2022935416

We are never as steeped in history as when we pretend not to be, but if we stop pretending we may gain in understanding what we lose in false innocence. Naïveté is often an excuse for those who exercise power. For those upon whom that power is exercised, naïveté is always a mistake.

—Michel-Rolph Trouillot

You know very well how they came to be there. When this world was dark with dirt and sand flying, and the stones were raised by the wind, and all were fighting with the government and themselves, you know very well how this thing happened. When all the nations came against us, then we lost our children.

—Manuelito

CONTENTS

CONTENTS

FOREWORD

When we Diné/Navajo meet, we often meet over food, and either a long-lasting friendship is developed, or we discover a family linkage through our clans and we establish a kinship. The author, Matt, and I exchanged e-mails in early 2020 and developed a plan to meet at one of my Diné weaving classes. We could not know that a month later, everything would shut down because of the COVID pandemic. We were thwarted a face-to-face meeting, but we kept up our communications by phone and e-mails to discuss the history of the Diné.

In my late mother's house, visitors were treated with her kind formality by being served food and coffee; small gifts were offered and stories were exchanged. As a teenager, I finally secured a spot at the grown-up table and was mesmerized by visitors, many of whom came from other countries. My late father was a trader at the Two Grey Hills Trading Post for thirty-five years, and he often brought tourists to visit our home in Newcomb, New Mexico, on the Navajo Nation, to observe my mother weaving. What still sticks in my mind is the different reactions of visitors when talk turned to our tribal history. Visitors from overseas knew more about the colonization of America than most Americans. They asked pointed questions, while Americans could only show shock and amazement, which by the way, still happens to this day. The whitewashed U.S. educational system robs us of the truth.

Matt has expressed time and time again how uneasy he feels about telling a part of our Diné history when he is not a tribal member. He has wondered:

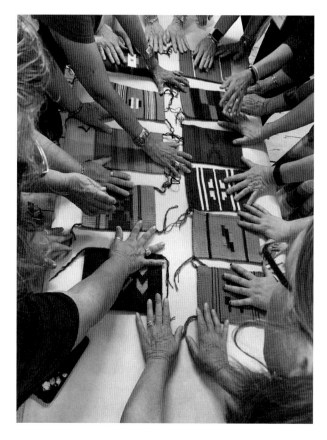

Students in a twenty-first-century Navajo weaving class bless their creations at Canyon de Chelly. *Lynda Teller Pete and Loom Dancer Odysseys.*

is he committing another act of colonialism? During these trying times, Americans—any caring human beings, really—need to know the truth. The horrible, unspeakable crimes of slavery, genocide and ethnic cleansing were perpetrated against all tribal nations from 1492 to 2022. What will it take to bring these to light, to be taught in schools and to be gleaned and learned from our remaining elders in our own languages? I am selective in reading books or listening to lectures from scholars and curators to add to my own work toward bringing corrections to Diné weaving history, and yes, it's true that I gravitate toward tribal authors, scholars, curators and conservationists who speak the truth. However, in my travels and the pursuit of my Diné history, we have allies who want the truth out there as much as we do. I place a high value on the author's determination to tell the true history by delving into historical papers and letters of those charged with the extermination and assimilation of the Diné. The narrative is changing. The renowned military heroes were the worst perpetrators of Diné slavery, and this book highlights the true Diné heroes who saved many of our ancestors. Some of our Diné heroes are Delgadito, Barboncito, Narbona, Armijo, Zarcillos Largos and Manuelito. But where are the Diné women? We are a matrilineal tribe, and with all the submitted military documentation, there is no mention of Diné women by name or by deeds. This is just the path of colonialism, leaving out the women who made history, but we know the heroes mentioned here had equal Diné women partners, grandmothers, mothers, aunts, sisters and daughters who assisted to protect the tribe. This is true; otherwise, I would not be here.

After the pandemic subsides, I hope to host my friend Matt at my table, to cement our journeys of correcting history; to enjoy the bounty from my garden, eating heritage squash and corn and the peach jam from the canyon peaches that survived the scorched-earth campaign of Kit Carson in Canyon de Chelly; and to show him photos of my seventh-generation Diné granddaughter weaving. We are still here!

—LYNDA TELLER PETE

PREFACE

Colonialism is a machine built to extract precious resources and to bury the truth as it goes. It's so big and efficient that it can be hard to recognize up close. Soldiers stationed on the western frontier referred to colonial times in the past tense. We still do it today, as if the Navajo Nation were not home to more than five hundred abandoned uranium mines, contaminating the land and water at this very moment. The earth has a way of opening up to remind us that the past is still present.

Yet many stories remain buried, especially those of women, who are all but invisible in the colonial archives. Navajo—or, more properly, Diné—oral histories make clear that women played leading roles in surviving the Long Walk, navigating internment at Bosque Redondo and negotiating the return to Dinétah. It's a matrilineal society, after all. In the writings of soldiers and territorial officials, however, women rarely appear except as victims or statistics.

Presented as a revisionist western, the story of Herrero Delgadito remains as bound by the limitations of gender as any of John Ford's old cavalry movies. Nevertheless, it is dedicated to three women: Mom, Jade and Natalie.

Many thanks are owed to Lynda Teller Pete and U.S. Army Major Patrick W. Naughton Jr. for their invaluable feedback, as well as to Adam Teller, Diné guide and oral historian, for setting the record straight.

PART I
BEAUTY BEFORE

THE PLACE WHERE TWO FELL OFF

Lieutenant Antonio Narbona, the man who was supposed to tame the Navajo, felt like a fool. "Overcome with mortification and shame," he wrote in December 1804, just three weeks after his arrival in New Mexico. He'd ridden north from Sonora with 215 men, provisions for sixty days and orders to avenge Navajo raids on a small frontier settlement called Cebolleta.[1] The village had been established a few years prior near the base of Blue Bead Mountain, one of four peaks the Navajo considered sacred, marking the boundaries of their country. Lieutenant Narbona's orders were to hit back at the tribe, to teach them the sanctity of Spanish land grants.

Two days of heavy snow blanketed the lieutenant's trail, causing him to miss a rendezvous with a second column of troops and spoiling plans for a two-pronged assault. His men cold, their horses spent, Lieutenant Narbona thought about turning around and just riding back to Sonora. He even worked out what it would take: five hundred pesos and supplies for twenty days.

But New Mexico's governor back then was Don Fernando Chacón, and the don had little patience for quitters. Just ask the settlers of Cebolleta, the town Narbona had been tasked to defend. When they tried to abandon the village, Chacón sent troops to intercept them, marching them back to Cebolleta under penalty of death.[2] So Lieutenant Narbona pressed on, into the very heart of Navajo country: Canyon de Chelly.

Even then, 250 years after the first conquistadors arrived in the region, Canyon de Chelly remained more legend than place. It had never been

Left: The Palace of the Governors in Santa Fe served as the seat of colonial power for Spain, Mexico and the United States. *Library of Congress.*

Opposite: For centuries, Spanish, Mexican and even American commanders warned against entering the yawning chasms of Canyon de Chelly. *Library of Congress.*

mapped, much less conquered. Few dared to approach the mysterious stronghold, its steep red walls rising three hundred, then five hundred and finally more than eight hundred feet overhead, while branching into a maze of secondary channels and dead ends. The name *de Chelly* was a Spanish corruption of the Navajo word *Tséyi'*, or "the place deep in the rock." It was the kind of place where a man could die without ever seeing who killed him.

Determined to breach the sandstone fortress, Lieutenant Narbona led his troops across another two hundred miles of snow and scrub. At last, they reached it. Visitors can still see their likenesses on one of the canyon walls, painted by a survivor. They're shown mounted on horseback, wearing wide-brimmed caps and carrying heavy-bore muskets, the cross of Christ emblazoned on an officer's cloak.

Spanish military archives include this brief account of what happened next: "January 25th, 1805, Lieut. Narbona reports from Zuñi a fight in the Canyon de Chelly, where he killed 90 men, 25 women and children, besides capturing 36 women and children; also 30 horses and 350 sheep."[3]

18

The soldiers returned to Santa Fe with proof of their victory, presenting Governor Chacón with eighty-four pairs of ears. Narbona apologized for losing the other six.[4] His reputation restored, the thirty-one-year-old lieutenant was destined to become governor of New Mexico himself one day.

The Navajo—or Diné, as they call themselves—tell a different version of events. They remember the snow, too, and how it was just starting to crust. At that time of year, the men always went hunting in the Lukachukai Mountains. Only women, children, elders and the lame were in the canyon that morning when someone shouted that the Spaniards were coming.

They all knew what to do. The women gathered everyone together and helped them make the climb to a hundred-foot-wide cave in the canyon wall. They called it the hiding cave. They'd been using it for years. They knew that their enemies were afraid to enter the mouth of the canyon, instead mounting attacks from the rim above. From up there, it was almost impossible to see the cave in the canyon wall. So that's where the Diné hid.

Once everyone was inside, some of the women took up positions in the rocks, so they could keep watch and sound the alarm. That night, they heard soldiers on the ridge above, the soft crush of hooves on snow accompanied by the squeak of saddle leather. They heard more men pass by, heading toward Spruce Creek. The sound receded. The Diné began to think they were safe.

That morning, the Spaniards appeared below them. They'd followed sheep tracks to a hidden trail, allowing them to descend to the canyon floor. From down there, they could see the cave in the canyon wall.

Unable to get a clear shot inside, the soldiers relied on ricochets. Marksmen positioned themselves on a high promontory to the west, guided by the soldiers below. They couldn't see beyond the entrance of the cave, so they began glancing musket balls off the far wall, scattering lead into the back of the cave, where they knew the people were huddled. They fired and reloaded over and over again. They could not see their targets—they could only hear their screams. It took a long time for the screams to stop.[5]

This account, passed down by generations of Diné, was corroborated more than a century after the killings when an American archaeologist and historian named Richard Van Valkenburgh climbed into the cave and documented its contents. Among the piles of bones, he found no sign of the ninety warriors the Spaniards claimed to have fought—just cradleboards, tiny moccasins and white pockmarks in the cave's wall. Using the name for the cave that appears on most maps today, he concluded, "With the evidence at hand from our visit to Massacre Cave, I am inclined to accept the Navajo version. The only men killed were the aged and crippled. All other victims were women and children."[6]

Diné oral histories recall that some survived the musket fire. It's said that one, an elderly man, hid himself and a few children under the dead. Another, an old woman, rushed the Spaniards when they entered the cave, carrying one of their officers over the ledge to the rocks below. This is why the Diné have another name for the cave: the Place Where Two Fell Off.

As news of Lieutenant Narbona's triumph spread through Spain's northern frontier, he sounded a note of caution, warning his comrades in Santa Fe against overconfidence:

> *I went through Canyon de Chelly, stronghold on which the Navajo have based their hopes of making themselves invincible, from its head to the mouth. Because many people live there and because nature has fortified it with the steep rock of which it is made, that hope is not ill-considered. Although I dislodged them this time, I can do no less than point out to you, as is my duty, and without exaggeration, that if in the future it is necessary to fight there again, a larger force than the one I had will be indispensable. They should take a large supply of munitions. I brought more than ten thousand rounds from my province, and had to use them all to get out of the canyon.*[7]

Hoping to subdue the Navajo once and for all, Governor Chacón demanded they sign a treaty. His initial terms were harsh, limiting Navajo territory and requiring them to return all livestock stolen during past raids. The governor offered one concession: the return of some Navajo women and children enslaved as household servants. It was a savvy negotiating move, as nothing mattered more to the Diné, with so many of their loved ones held captive in the Spanish settlements.

Though never legal in New Mexico, the enslavement of Native Americans had been openly tolerated for as long as anyone remembered. Sales were rarely recorded, but parish priests baptized many of the captives, leaving a paper trail all the way back to 1694. Analyzing Catholic Church records, the anthropologist/archaeologist David M. Brugge determined that by the early 1800s, most of the families living in Santa Fe kept slaves. Out of 794 households, 711 held at least one Native captive. Eighty-three households held three or more people in bondage; some held a dozen.[8] Settlers avoided calling them slaves, referring to them as *criados*, or servants, instead. Most were women or children.

The Diné also took captives in raids, as did most of the Indigenous nations in the region, but not in numbers comparable to the colonizers. In 1805, the year of the Canyon de Chelly massacre, the Navajo Nation's population was at least twelve thousand. Yet when negotiating for the release of their own people that year, Diné leaders were only able to produce two Spanish captives, both children.

Chacón initially proposed an even swap: since the Navajo held only two captives, they'd receive only two women in exchange. Fortunately for the

Untold generations of Diné families have tended crops alongside the ancient ruins of Canyon de Chelly and Canyon del Muerto. *Library of Congress.*

Diné, Chacón was replaced as governor before the terms were finalized. His successor, Joaquín del Real Alencaster, took a softer position. In the end, seventeen captives were returned in exchange for the two Spanish children.[9]

It must have been a bittersweet homecoming, given how many more women and children remained enslaved in the settlements. Spanish troops reported taking three dozen captives in the last expedition alone. Nevertheless, the Diné agreed to stop mounting raids on Cebolleta, having been promised they'd be left in peace, under the protection of the king.

THE FORGE OF CEBOLLETA

When consciousness returned, Manuel Chaves found himself deep inside Navajo country, surrounded by the dead. It was night; his clothes were wet. Soaked in his own blood, he realized, seeping from five…six…seven arrow wounds. At least he could move.

Something else moved—a boy, one of Cebolleta's young slaves, injured and hiding in the rocks. Barely sixteen himself, Manuel ordered the boy to come help him. They worked together, pulling at the rocks and sand until at last they'd dug a shallow grave for Manuel's older brother Jose. Another dozen or so bodies lay nearby. The two young survivors would leave those where they fell before starting the two-hundred-mile walk back home.[10]

The year was 1834. The company had set out from Cebolleta several days earlier, with Jose Chaves at the head. It was Manuel's first expedition, a rite of passage of sorts, his chance to learn from his brother how to capture Navajo women and children.

The slave trade that took root in New Mexico under Spain expanded after Mexican revolutionaries rose to power in the 1820s, with wealthy, established settlers like the Chaves brothers leading the charge. As the westernmost colony, Cebolleta had emerged as the tip of the spear for incursions into Navajo country. A thick stone wall, ten feet high, enclosed the entire town. The only entrance was sealed by a narrow gate, constructed from two mammoth pine timbers and fastened by a sturdy iron bar.[11] It protected the settlers—and imprisoned their abductees.

ACROSS THE CONTINENT ON THE KANSAS PACIFIC RAILROAD.

(ROUTE OF THE 35TH PARALLEL.)

Mexican Town of Cubero, New Mexico, Western Outpost on 35th Parallel,

935 MILES WEST OF MISSOURI RIVER.

No. 74.

Settlers in villages like Cebolleta and Cubero, shown here during the 1860s, enslaved Natives as household servants. Children were preferred, especially girls. *Boston Public Library.*

Church archives show at least 451 Diné captives were baptized in local parishes during the first half of the nineteenth century.[12] Not every captive was baptized, but many were, often within days or weeks of their abduction. Baptizing captives served two purposes. It provided a religious justification for seizing Indigenous children in the first place and also a preemptive argument against returning them later, since to do so could be portrayed as a separation from God.

Of course, the slavers already had done just that—they tore their Navajo captives from the prayers, teachings, songs and stories that had sustained their people for generations. Forced to kneel at the baptismal font, Diné prisoners were stripped of everything that made them who they were, down to the names their families gave them.

Slavers—and the slavers of Cebolleta in particular—were celebrated by their fellow settlers. In years to come, Manuel Chaves would become associated with one of the worst atrocities of the U.S. "Indian Wars." Back in 1834, however, when the region was still under Mexican control, the bloody details of his first slaving expedition made him a hero throughout the territory.

His party had scoured the countryside for days, hoping to find a small group of Navajo they could overpower. The plan was always the same: kill the men and take the women and children captive. The slave boy, captured on some past raid, was most likely brought along to translate.

When they finally reached Canyon de Chelly, they stumbled on a massive Diné gathering defended by hundreds of warriors. Struck in the chest by an arrow, the slave boy hid until it was over, and he stayed hidden, even after the sun went down. He might have stayed like that all night if Manuel hadn't opened his eyes and started moving around.

After they buried Manuel's brother, the pair began walking back to Cebolleta. It took them two days and two nights to reach Bear Springs, a well-known watering hole. They stopped there for the evening. Manuel waded into the pool to wash his wounds; remarkably, none of the arrows had lodged in bone or injured vital organs. The young Navajo was not so fortunate. Manuel woke the next morning to discover that the boy had died. He continued on alone.

He still had miles to go when he encountered some Mexican shepherds. They loaded the wounded youth onto a litter and carried him the rest of the way home, into the welcoming arms of Cebolleta. "El Leoncito," they called him. "The Little Lion."

Manuel had another brother, named Pedro. The oldest of the three, Pedro was an experienced slaver, and Jose's death only seemed to spur him on. Throughout the 1830s and 1840s, he continued to mount expeditions into Navajo country, abducting scores of women and children. Charles F. Lummis, a journalist and family friend, reported:

> *Pedro Chaves (oldest brother of Manuel) used to go to the Rio Grande settlements and take contracts from those in need of domestic "help," to furnish them with Navajo girls at five hundred dollars per head. Then he would get his fellow Cebolletans together, and they would start out on a campaign, strike a band of Navajoes, kill the warriors, and bring the women and children home for servants. The rivalry among the young men to prove their courage led to exploits no whit behind the doughtiest of chivalric*

deeds. It was no uncommon thing for a young Cebolletan warrior to spur ahead of the company, seize a Navajo warrior by the hair, and try to drag him from his horse and bring him back alive, recklessness which sometimes succeeded.[13]

The story was much the same at other settlements, from Cubero to Abiquiú. By the 1840s, it was not unusual for hundreds of people to join in private slaving expeditions. In January 1850, a Mexican prefect named Don Ramon Luna organized an expedition of one thousand volunteers.[14]

And yet, sometime in the early 1850s, a young Diné man lifted himself onto his horse and struck out alone for Cebolleta. He was still in his twenties, with a compact frame and wiry limbs. No one knows what he was called back then. The first name that Diné babies receive is spiritual in nature, often known only to the immediate family and rarely uttered after death. Public names come later and, in those days, often changed with time and circumstance. A child called Slim Girl might grow up to be Woman Who Owns the Stone House.

Today, military historians remember the Navajo rider by the name Herrero Delgadito, Spanish for "Skinny Little Blacksmith." Scattered through U.S. Army archives is the story of how he helped to lead the Navajo Nation into exile and back out the other side.

In the Native arts world, he is known by the last of his Diné names, Atsidí Sání, or "Old Pounder." Some say that he was the first Navajo silversmith, the one who taught others the craft, fathering an art form now prized the world over. His true legacy may be even greater than that, as a diplomat, medicine man, insurgent and counterfeiter, too, running a ring that duplicated thousands of U.S. Army ration tickets at a time of mass starvation.

Born into the Coyote Pass People clan, Delgadito was raised with his brothers, Barboncito and Sordo, in the protective embrace of Canyon del Muerto, a massive, secondary branch of Canyon de Chelly.[15] Life was driven by the seasons and the teachings of the holy ones. In good years, the corn grew tall and the pumpkins nice and fat.

Thousands of peach trees grew in the canyons too. Tens of thousands of sheep grazed in the surrounding countryside. The women wove beautiful blankets to keep the children warm when the cottonwoods turned yellow and the rabbit trails headed south.

Their band numbered about five hundred in those days. Barboncito and Sordo were natural leaders, each in his own way. Barboncito's eloquence and intelligence earned him the Diné name Hastiin Daagi Bistłahałání, or "The

Great Orator." Sordo was a warrior through and through; they called him 'Ádiníhę̨ę̨' Nééz, or "The Tall One Who Hates People of Another Color."[16] Delgadito was not the fiercest warrior or the most gifted speaker. But he was bright, curious and entrepreneurial, and it occurred to him that he still had something to offer.

It was iron, not silver, that first led Delgadito down to Cebolleta. One of his future protégés, the silversmith Grey Moustache, recalled:

> *He thought that he could earn money by making bridles. In those days the Navajo bought all of their bridles from the Mexicans, and Atsidí Sání thought that if he learned how to make them, the Navajo would buy them from him. So he went down to the region of Mt. Taylor, and there he watched this Mexican smith at work.*[17]

It was a risky bet that Delgadito made, striking out for a town full of enemies. But this was his country, after all, not theirs. The mountain that loomed over Cebolleta was one of four sacred peaks that defined the boundaries of Dinétah. The holy ones had placed the mountains, and the rivers too, to protect the Diné and to mark their borders for all to see.

Perhaps, as Delgadito rode south toward Cebolleta and Blue Bead Mountain, he also sensed an opening, a chance to break free from the endless cycles of violence. For one thing, Pedro Chaves was dead, killed by Diné warriors while returning from a raid in 1850.[18] But more important, Chaves's fellow Cebolletans were now taking orders from the New Men.

The New Men called themselves Americans. They'd stormed in from the east in the late 1840s, and they achieved what Diné warriors could not, driving the despised Mexican military out of New Mexico. Naturally, some of the Diné wondered if it might signal an end to the years of raids and reprisals. Perhaps it would even bring an end to the slave trade.

Few could have imagined how much worse it would become.

NEW MEN

J ames S. Calhoun, New Mexico Territory's first Indian agent, didn't know much about either the territory or its Indians. A Georgia politician who ran a shipping business on the side, he had one main qualification: he was a diehard Whig, just like Zachary Taylor, the newly elected president of the United States.[19]

If Calhoun was hoping for guidance from Washington, he was out of luck. Upon his appointment in April 1849, U.S. Commissioner of Indian Affairs William Medill informed him, "So little is known here of the condition and situation of the Indians in that region, that no specific instructions relative to them can be given at present."[20]

The Americans' ignorance was understandable, considering how fast things happened. It had only been a year since the U.S. Army of the West marched down to Mexico City and forced the government there to surrender 55 percent of its territory. New Mexico—along with what we now call Arizona, Colorado, Utah, Nevada and California—became American soil overnight.

The question of slavery was roiling Congress and the states back then. The nation was evenly divided between fifteen free states and fifteen slave states. From the moment New Mexico became a U.S. holding, it was viewed as a prize in the wider struggle. Texans—growing rich in cotton and reliant on slavery—started talking about annexing parts of New Mexico, expanding their borders and legalized slavery in one move.

President Taylor, a hero of the Mexican-American War, in whose honor Blue Bead Mountain was renamed Mount Taylor, envisioned free states in the West. Though a slave owner himself, he sent Calhoun to Santa Fe to build support for New Mexico statehood in a bid to block the spread of southern-style plantation slavery.

With little understanding of the territory or the illicit slave trade that infested it, Calhoun viewed the Hispano settlers as natural allies. The 1848 treaty with Mexico made them U.S. citizens, after all, and Calhoun was counting on their votes for a state constitution.

And so, in order to stop the spread of legalized slavery from Texas, federal officials aligned themselves with the slaveholding settlers of New Mexico. They placed the blame for the territory's longstanding violence squarely on the Navajo, denouncing their character before they'd even settled on a spelling of their name. Just weeks after arriving in the territory, Calhoun wrote:

> *The Navajoes commit their wrongs from a pure love of rapine and plunder....*
> *They derive their title to the country over which they roam from mere possession,*
> *not knowing from whence they came, or how they were planted upon its soil;*
> *and its soil is easy of cultivation, and capable of sustaining nearly as many*
> *millions of inhabitants as they have thousands. I respectfully suggest, these*
> *people should have their limits circumscribed, and distinctly marked out, and*
> *their departure from said limits should be under certain prescribed rules, at*
> *least for some time to come. Even this arrangement would be utterly ineffective*
> *unless enforced by the military arm of the country.*
>
> *These Indians are hardy, and intelligent, and it is as natural for them to*
> *war against all men, and to take the property of others, as it is for the sun*
> *to give light by day.*[21]

Calhoun's rush to judgment is particularly striking given the complexity of the region, with its shifting web of alliances, animosities and agendas. Major Patrick W. Naughton Jr., a U.S. Army historian and Iraq War veteran who analyzed the military operating environment in New Mexico Territory during that period, uncovered a tangle of loyalties and grudges similar to what U.S. troops encounter overseas today. In a 2018 paper submitted to the U.S. Army Command and General Staff College, Naughton wrote:

> *The area surrounding Santa Fe, Mexico in 1846 mirrored the cultural*
> *environments that American forces find themselves in presently; namely,*

populations consisting of various groups engaged in persistent localized conflicts, each with their own desires and agendas. As in the contemporary cultural milieu of Iraq and Afghanistan, military leaders are often not aware of the complex societal frameworks and underlying tensions they are functioning in....Upon the arrival of the Army of the West in 1846, the Navajo were immediately painted as the primary nuisance and enemy by all sides in the region....When examining the primary source documents relating to the conflict in the region, it quickly becomes obvious that the Navajo were seen differently than the other native groups. Each exchange is hostile and accusatory in its context.[22]

No community stood apart from the region's violence. The Pueblos to the east and the Ute bands up north also engaged in raids and reprisals. And for as long as anyone could remember, the various combatants made it a practice to seize women and children as captives, Diné warriors included.

It was different with Hispano and Ute raiders. For them, taking captives was not just an aspect of frontier warfare—it became the whole point. By the 1830s, they'd turned it into an industry. Though frequent targets of slave raids themselves, some Ute bands relocated south to be closer to the communities they raided and the settlers to whom they sold captives.[23] The Navajo bore the brunt of attacks from settlers and Ute raiders alike. Their children, particularly the girls, were considered ideal servants and commanded the highest price at market.[24]

What confused the Diné most was the American claim that their common enemy—the Mexicans—were now Americans too. Under the terms of the 1848 treaty with Mexico, the Spanish-speaking settlers in annexed territories gained the rights of U.S. citizens, including the protection of the U.S. military. The American army didn't even wait to conquer the territory before issuing its first warnings to the Navajo in 1846. Zarcillos Largos, one of the senior headmen, responded:

Americans! You have a strange cause of war against the Navajos. We have waged war against New Mexicans for several years. We have plundered their villages and killed many of their people, and made many prisoners. We had just cause for all this. You have lately commenced a war against the same people. You are powerful. You have great guns and many brave soldiers. You have therefore conquered them, the very thing we have been attempting to do for so many years. You now turn upon us for attempting to do what you have done yourselves. We cannot see why you have cause of quarrel with us for fighting the New Mexicans on the west, while you do the same thing on the east. Look how matters stand. This is our war. We have more right to complain of you interfering in our war, than you have to quarrel with us for continuing a war we had begun long before you got here. If you will act justly, you will allow us to settle our own differences.[25]

The Americans had no intention of letting that happen. Just days after arriving in the territory, Calhoun set out with Brevet Lieutenant Colonel John Washington on the United States' first full-fledged military expedition into Navajo country. The objective was a treaty, but the participants didn't seem to view it as a peace mission. Their map was titled "Expedition Against the Navajos Indians."

Colonel Washington, who served as the territory's military governor before the establishment of a civil government, brought along four hundred troops, three mountain howitzers and a six-pound field gun that his soldiers called the "thunderwagon."

Even so, some Diné wondered if the arrival of the New Men might be a good thing. Their warriors had spent decades fighting the Mexicans. Now these Americans brushed them aside like leaves—was it possible they would free the Diné held captive in the settlements?

Calhoun and Washington had exactly the opposite in mind. The treaty they envisioned called on the Navajo to release any Hispano captives they'd taken but said nothing of returning Dinétah's stolen sons, daughters, wives and mothers.[26]

Unsure where the Americans stood, the Diné were encouraged to meet by one of their most revered leaders, an old warrior whom the colonizers called Narbona, although, of course, he was not related to the Spanish officer of that name. Narbona's Navajo names are lost to history, but his reputation as a resistance leader is well remembered. He fought invaders across six decades, dealing the Mexicans their greatest defeat in 1835. The Diné ambushed one thousand soldiers that year in a steep mountain pass, killing most of them.

In 1849, Colonel Washington's men marched through the very same pass; American mapmakers promptly commemorated the event by naming it "Washington Pass." Narbona was about eighty years old when Colonel Washington's troops arrived in Navajo country. Having seen so much war, he advised his fellow Diné to give these New Men a chance.

Hundreds of people, women and children included, arrived with Narbona at the American camp around noon on August 31. Lieutenant James Simpson, the expedition's surveyor, described Narbona in his journal as "quite old and of

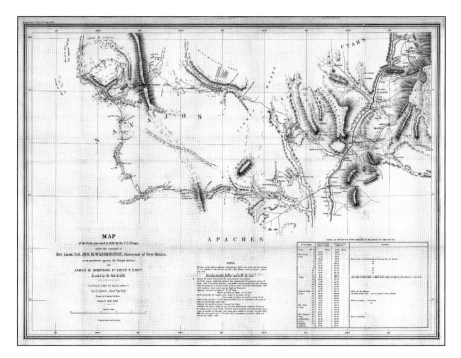

Above: The map of the 1849 expedition, drawn by Lieutenant James Simpson, makes no mention of the killing of the revered Diné leader Narbona. *Author's collection*.

Right: The Diné leader Narbona as he appeared at the 1849 treaty negotiations, shortly before he was killed and scalped by U.S. troops. *Amon Carter Museum*.

a very large frame, having a grave and contemplative countenance not unlike, as many of the officers remarked (I hope the comparison will be pardoned), that of President Washington."[27]

The meeting seemed to be going well. Narbona made clear that he did not speak for all the Diné; there were many different bands, living in different parts of the nation, and each could speak for itself. Nevertheless, Narbona and a few other headmen agreed to send representatives to a second council planned for Canyon de Chelly, where a treaty would be signed.[28]

Just as things were winding down, someone accused a Diné man of riding a stolen horse. Colonel Washington demanded the animal be returned. When it wasn't surrendered, he ordered his men to seize both mount and rider. Calhoun recalled:

> *The moment the guard was ordered forward, every Navajo Indian in the crowd, supposed to number from three to four hundred, all mounted and armed, and their arms in their hands, wheeled, and put the spur to their horses; upon which, the Governor ordered the guard to fire.*[29]

The soldiers opened up with rifles, followed by three blasts from the thunderwagon. When the smoke cleared, Narbona and a half dozen others lay dead. Someone stepped forward with a knife—a New Mexican volunteer, one of the territory's newly minted American citizens—and sliced off the old man's scalp.[30]

Not seeming to grasp what had just happened, Colonel Washington ordered his men to continue on to Canyon de Chelly, to sign the treaty as scheduled. Lieutenant Simpson wrote of his excitement to map "the fabled Navajo presidio." Not surprisingly, when they reached the canyon a few days later, the Diné kept their distance, observing the Americans from high ledges.

A Diné man named Mariano Martinez finally approached on September 7. Colonel Washington told him that the Navajo must sign the treaty to avoid war. Martinez returned two days later with another Diné man. As a gesture of goodwill, the men brought along 104 sheep, some burros and four Mexican captives, offering to turn them all over. Calhoun described the four captives in his report:

> *Anto Josea about 10 years old, taken from Jemez where his parents now live, by the Navajo, who delivered him. A flock of Goats & Sheep were stolen at the same time. He says he was well treated.*

> *Teodosia Gonzales, twelve years of age, was taken about six years ago, from a corral near the Rio Grande, where he supposes his parents now live. He was stolen while herding goats, but no effort was made to take the goats. He was well treated.*
>
> *Marceito, eighteen years of age, was taken from Socorro. He knows nothing of his parents, nor how long he has been captive. He has evidently been a captive many years, as he has entirely forgotten his native tongue. The novelty of a home, as explained to him, seemed to excite him somewhat.*
>
> *Josea Ignacio Anañe, became a prisoner seventeen years ago, taken, when quite a boy, by a roving band of Navajoes at Tuckalotoe. His parents then lived at Santa Fe, where he supposes they now reside. He is the fortunate possessor of two wives, and three children, living at Mecina Gorda (Big Oak), north of Cheille two and a half days travel. He was originally sold to an Indian named Waro, to whom he yet belongs. I do not think he is under many restraints, for he prefers most decidedly to remain with the Navajoes, notwithstanding his peonage.*[31]

According to Calhoun, the captives were later returned to people who knew their families, "except the one so fortunately married." The treaty of 1849 was signed that morning, without any reference to the hundreds of Diné who remained enslaved in Spanish-speaking settlements. Approved by the Senate a year later to the day, it remains one of only two treaties with the Navajo Nation ever ratified by Congress.

It was a waste of paper, irrelevant before it was signed. It was absurd to think that the marks of two men, made under such circumstances, would bind an entire nation. And perhaps that was the whole idea. Writing in his journal, Lieutenant Simpson suggested that the Americans were preparing a justification for war:

> *It is true the Navahos may fail to comply with treaty. But whether they comply or not, the fact still remains the same, that a treaty covering the whole ground of their fealty…was necessary in order to satisfy the public mind, as well as testify to the whole world that should any future coercion become necessary, it would be but a just retribution and, in a manner, their own act.*[32]

The bias against the Navajo was not universal. In 1851, as the territory transitioned from military to civilian rule, Calhoun was appointed its new governor. A man named John Greiner was picked to take Calhoun's place as the territorial Indian agent. Greiner was no more qualified for the job than Calhoun had been, and he said so himself a little over a decade later when called before a Congressional committee:

The great difficulty in our Indian policy is in the selection of Indian agents, who are generally appointed for political services. Mr. Wingfield came here as an agent, because he was the friend of Mr. Dawson, of Georgia; Mr. Wolley, an old man of seventy years of age, because he was the friend of Mr. Clay; Mr. Weighman, because he wished to be returned as delegate; and myself, because I could sing a good political song. Neither of us was by habit or education better fitted to be Indian agent than to follow any other business. The general policy of selecting men as agents for political services, rather than fitness for the position, and frequently changing them, is a great cause of all our Indian difficulties, in my opinion. I was changed just as I was about to be of service, and had become acquainted with the Indians, and had acquired their confidence, and could get them to do as I desired.[33]

Fair-minded and straight-talking, Greiner was one of the few Americans who raised hopes among the Diné that these New Men might truly represent something new. In January 1852, he traveled to a spot near Jemez to meet with the senior headman, Armijo. Barboncito attended too. They all took a seat, and Armijo spoke first:

Armijo: I have been a captain ever since I was a young man. I have come to tell my Great Father that my people wish to live in peace and quiet. We wish to cultivate the soil, as our fathers did before us, to have the water run through our acequias so that we may irrigate our lands. We do not wish to be molested. We have to depend upon our fingernails and our toenails for support. By the labor of our own hands, we wish to raise our own crops, and like the sun we wish to follow the course of nature. The bows and arrows we carry are to shoot game with, the deer, the antelope, and the rabbit. But little rain fell from the clouds last year, our crops failed, and our young men have to support our families by hunting.

I have lost my grandfather and two other members of my family, who were all killed by Mexicans. I have never sought revenge. My hair is beginning to get gray; I wish to live in peace with everyone. I want to see my cattle and horses to be well grazed and my sheep to be safely herded—and to get fat—which can never be done while my people are at war. We like the Americans. We have eaten their bread and meat and smoked their tobacco;

the clothing they have given us has kept us warm in the cold winter and the snow. With the hoes they have given us we will cultivate our land. We are struck dead with gratitude. I am now before you—you can all see me, my name is well known everywhere. My people are better dressed than I am myself, and although I am ashamed to appear before you so poorly clad, I wished you to see me just as I am, to tell you I can plant corn and wheat, and raise food for my people to eat. If the [spirits] will supply us with plenty of clouds, we shall walk about our lands, and feel satisfied.

Greiner: My brothers, let us talk plain so that we understand each other. The people living in the Rio Abajo complain that the Navajos have captured their children, stolen their stock—that their fields have to be idle for they cannot work them for fear of your people. Is this not so?

Armijo: My people are all crying in the same way. Three of our chiefs now sitting before you mourn for their children, who have been taken from their homes by the Mexicans. More than 200 of our children have been carried off and we know not where they are. The Mexicans have lost but few children in comparison with what they have stolen from us.…Eleven times have we given up our captives, only once have they given us ours. My people are yet crying for the children they have lost. Is it American justice that we must give up everything, and receive nothing?

Greiner: You have never told us this before. The Great Father at Washington shall hear of it—and you shall hear what he says.[34]

Greiner was being disingenuous; by then, he and other American commanders were well aware of the slave trade. Still, he meant what he said about informing his superiors in Washington. Greiner passed along everything Armijo had said, along with this note:

There is too much truth in what these Indians complain of—it was the custom of the Mexicans to fit out expeditions against them, everyone claiming what he stole as his plunder. They own large flocks of sheep, goats, horses, mules, and cattle. They are a very industrious, hard-working people. They not only till their lands themselves, but they manufacture their own clothing—and a Navajo blanket will at any time command the price of a mule. It is not to be wondered at if they should retaliate, when they so repeatedly suffered by these marauding expeditions. These Indians are now what the U.S. Government is striving to make of all the Wild Indian tribes—a farming community. I was so well convinced with the truth of the remarks of Armijo, that I confess I had but little to say. If the Indians must return all the captives and property taken from the Mexicans, is it anything but just that they should claim what has been stolen from them? I think not.

So, in the early 1850s, around the time Herrero Delgadito untethered his horse and rode south toward Cebolleta, it was still unclear where the Americans stood, even among themselves. It was a gambit riding down there alone. A new flag might fly over the Cebolleta barracks, but the slave raiders still lived behind its high stone wall—including Manuel Chaves, the Little Lion of Cebolleta.

As Delgadito approached the fortified village, it's likely that he kept to the trail, making sure he was seen and making sure that everyone in Cebolleta knew he wanted to be seen. Nice and easy, so no one did anything rash.

By now, it was a good bet that somewhere in Cebolleta, someone was watching Delgadito, taking the measure of this unfamiliar Navajo on the far side of the wall, coming up the trail at a slow gait. The Navajo were practically raised on horseback, and the people of Cebolleta were raised to fear them. Just imagine the settlers' surprise when one rode into town, looking for the village blacksmith.

HERRERO

All through the 1850s and early 1860s, the U.S. Army compiled lists of prominent Diné men. Officers ranked the names in a hierarchy of their own imagination, seeking to identify a single "principal chief" with whom they could negotiate. There was no such person. Scattered over a vast country, organized in distinct clans and believing that individuals have a right to choose their own path, the Diné answered to themselves. Still, the Americans refused to give up and, years later, would go so far as to designate their own "head chief."

Art historians did pretty much the same thing in their quest to identify the "first Navajo silversmith." Eventually, they settled on Herrero Delgadito, aka Atsidí Sání, as the person who started it all. They based their conclusion on a handful of interviews conducted in the 1930s and 1940s with men like Grey Moustache, one of the silversmiths whom Delgadito mentored. Grey Moustache recalled:

> Atsidí Sání was my father's uncle by marriage; he married my grandmother's sister. He was the first Navajo to learn how to make silver, and my grandmother told me that he had learned how to work with iron before that. He learned how to do this from a Mexican by the name of Nakai Tsosi (Thin Mexican) who lived down near Mt. Taylor....This smith didn't charge him anything for teaching him how to work iron. I remember watching Atsidí Sání make bridle bits out of pieces of scrap iron. He made them with jingles hanging from the bottom.[35]

Two early books on silversmithing—Arthur Woodward's *Navajo Silver* (1938) and John Adair's *The Navajo and Pueblo Silversmiths* (1944)—identified Delgadito as the likely father of the form. Today, the claim is copied and pasted onto gallery web pages as a matter of fact, no longer qualified as recollections that someone formed in childhood, in the aftermath of war and exile.

At the time Grey Moustache was interviewed, just two generations removed from the Long Walk, Delgadito was still a towering figure in the minds of many Diné. It's not surprising that Delgadito would be credited with forging a new future. He certainly was the most important of the early smiths, for reasons that had nothing to do with being first.

Army intelligence reports underscore the challenge in trying to pin down when and where it all began. The fluidity of Diné names means that as people acquired new skills, some also acquired new names. Herrero—Spanish for "blacksmith"—shows up regularly in reports of the 1850s and 1860s. Without realizing it, soldiers were documenting the rise of an industry. Forges were lighting up all over Dinétah.

Herrero Chiquito, Herrero Grande, Herrero Viejo and Herrero 2nd all appear in army intelligence reports. A December 1860 report by Colonel Edward Canby, the territory's top commander, listed "Herrero No. 1" and "Herrero No. 2." Canby added in a footnote, "The elder Herrero possesses a great deal of influence with the Navajoes, on account of his trade, and from the fact he is a medicine man."[36]

If Canby was referring to Herrero Delgadito, his assessment was correct. By the mid-1850s, Delgadito had become a headman—someone people came to for advice and to mediate disputes. He'd also studied to be a medicine man, becoming a practitioner of the Shooting Way and Mountain Way ceremonies.[37]

Delgadito's skill with metal had earned him large flocks of sheep and herds of horses, which he grazed on the rolling mesas west of Canyon de Chelly.[38] He shared what he knew with others, showing younger smiths how to construct a good forge and how to use turkey feathers to fan that first small flame into a workable fire. Many of the early silversmiths learned from him, including four of his own sons: Big Black, Red Smith, Little Smith and Burnt Whiskers.[39]

Art historians and gallery owners tend to point to the 1870s as the genesis of Navajo silversmithing, after the Diné returned from forced exile. Grey Moustache similarly reported that Delgadito worked iron for several years before exploring silver. Records of the era, however, show that Navajo

Americans arriving in New Mexico Territory in the 1850s observed—and, in this case, sketched—Navajo silver fashioned into bridles, belts and more. *Author's collection.*

silversmiths had mastered the craft by the 1850s at the latest. Diné men— including Delgadito—were observed wearing silver belts and other items before they were forced into exile by the U.S. government in the 1860s.[40] The first detailed illustration of a silver concho belt appeared in an 1858 U.S. Army report on a survey the Colorado River. An intricate bridle is also shown, with jingles hanging off it, just as Grey Moustache described.[41]

William Watts Hart Davis, a writer and historian who held multiple posts in the territorial government, visited Navajo country in 1855 to attend a council with Delgadito and other Diné headmen. He reported:

> *They manufacture all their own wearing apparel, and make their arms, such as bows, arrows, and lances; they also weave a beautiful article of blankets, and knit woolen stockings.…The skin breeches come down to the knee, where they are met by blue stockings that cover the lower half of the leg; the breeches fit tight around the limbs, and the outer seams are adorned with silver or brass buttons. The coat reaches below the hips, with a hole at the top to thrust the head through, and open at the sides; it is made of wool, woven in bright colors, and is fastened at the waist by a leather belt,*

highly ornamented with silver when the wearer can afford it. They wear numerous strands of fine coral, and many valuable belts of silver, and generally appear with a handsome blanket thrown over their side, in the style of a mantel.

The Nabajo [sic] is seldom seen on foot, a horse being as indispensable to him as an Arab of the desert. They manufacture their own saddles and bridles, bits, stirrups, etc., as also the looms on which they weave their handsome blankets, which are quite an ingenious affair.[42]

The notion that Diné smiths mastered iron in the 1850s but waited decades to work silver has never made much sense. Silver is easier to melt and shape than iron, and it was literally the currency of the day, tossed around the territory in a variety of coins, chief among them Mexico's eight-reales peso. The monetary descendant of Spanish "pieces of eight," Mexican pesos were prized for their consistency by monarchs and pirates alike. Minted from 27.07 grams of .903 fine silver, the peso dominated international trade throughout the 1850s, serving as the standard for exchange in seaports from Galveston to Guangzhou.[43]

It wasn't just Diné men turning colonial coins into Native art. Women worked silver too. Gus Bighorse, a young warrior who briefly rode with Delgadito in the 1860s, recalled that his mother was a silversmith before she was killed by U.S. forces in 1863.[44]

From tools to techniques, Diné smiths engineered an entirely new approach to the craft. They stoked their fires with goatskin bellows, they poured silver into sandstone molds and—unlike their Hispano, Pueblo and Anglo counterparts—they found a way to make the whole process portable.

Washington Matthews, an army surgeon who became fascinated with silversmithing while stationed at Fort Wingate in the 1880s, noted that only Diné smiths built temporary forges rather than permanent ones. This gave them the unique ability to practice their trade anywhere:

I once engaged two of the best workmen in the tribe to come to Fort Wingate and work under my observation for a week. They put up their forge in a small outbuilding at night, and early next morning they were at work. Their labor was almost all performed while they were sitting or crouching on the ground in very constrained positions; yet I never saw men who worked harder or more steadily. They often labored from twelve to fifteen hours a day, eating their meals with dispatch and returning to their toil the moment they had done. Occasionally they stopped to roll a

A Diné silversmith at work. This photo, taken around 1915 by William Carpenter, shows that Mexican pesos remained a source of silver into the twentieth century. *Library of Congress.*

> *cigarette or consult about their work, but they lost very few moments in this way. They worked by the job and their prices were such that they earned about two dollars a day each.*[45]

Dr. Matthews was not the first American to take an interest in Diné smithing. Thirty years earlier, another had been keen to watch them work. He went so far as to give them tools and iron.[46] Before long, he was spending more time with them than with his fellow Americans. In three centuries of colonialism, the Diné had never encountered anyone like this man.

His name was Henry Lafayette Dodge—"Red Shirt," the Navajo called him. He and Delgadito would soon cross paths as their countries tumbled toward war.

RED SHIRT

James Calhoun, New Mexico Territory's first Indian agent and first civilian governor, departed Santa Fe for the States in May 1852, riding ahead of a wagon loaded with two tents, two water tanks and his own coffin.

Calhoun had been ill almost since the day he arrived. By the time he finally quit the territory, he suspected that he might not make it home to Georgia. Just outside Independence, Missouri, it turned out he was right.[47]

Calhoun never succeeded in securing statehood for New Mexico. California was admitted as a free state, but on the condition that it send to Washington one proslavery senator and one antislavery senator, to maintain the balance. The compromise also called for New Mexico to remain a territory. Without a state constitution to ban slavery or any laws that formally legalized it, the question of slavery remained as unresolved in New Mexico as it did in the nation as a whole.

Before Calhoun left Santa Fe, he appointed John Greiner the new acting superintendent of Indian affairs. Greiner's first day on the job, he scheduled a meeting with Henry L. Dodge, a civilian appointee who had a reputation for working miracles with Natives.

Dodge was Calhoun's opposite in many ways. Where Calhoun was an upright and officious southerner, Dodge was a free-spirited (some would say reckless) midwesterner. Calhoun had built a successful shipping business from scratch; Dodge was born to money and power, the black sheep of one of America's most famous frontier families.

Dodge's father, U.S. Senator Henry Dodge, was a hero of the Black Hawk War who guided Wisconsin to statehood as its last territorial governor. When Dodge's younger brother, Augustus Caesar Dodge, was elected as one of Iowa's first senators in 1846, it marked the first and only time a father and son served concurrent terms in the U.S. Senate.

Henry Dodge's trajectory was less impressive. At the time of his brother's election, he was a thirty-six-year-old district court clerk in Iowa County, Wisconsin, raising four young children with his wife, Adele. And then one day, he wasn't. Henry L. Dodge disappeared that year, leaving behind his family, his legal practice, his personal reputation—everything.[48]

He resurfaced in Santa Fe three months later, balancing the books as the territory's newly appointed treasurer. It was an odd position for a man who was loose with money and hated paperwork. Yet it was on the frontier, in a land more exotic than any his father or brother had seen. Santa Fe's plazas hummed with a half dozen languages. Spanish dominated, but as he walked the streets, Dodge also heard the languages of the Pueblos: Tewa, Tiwa, Keresan and even Hopi.

Then there were the soldiers. The ranks of the Regular Army were filled with men from every part of the country, as well as immigrants from across Europe, Germans and Irish most of all. Dodge—curious, approachable and quick with a joke—got along fine with most of them.

In 1849, Dodge formed a company of volunteers in support of Colonel Washington's expedition into Navajo country, serving as its captain. He was out on a scouting detail when Washington ordered his men to open fire on the Navajo delegation, killing their leader, Narbona. When Dodge arrived on the scene a while later, his unit came under fire from jittery U.S. troops, narrowly escaping injury.[49]

Later that year, American commanders decided to station soldiers in Cebolleta, moving them into barracks previously occupied by Spanish and Mexican troops. Dodge was among several civilians drafted into supporting roles. Assigned to manage the post's supplies, he began venturing beyond Cebolleta, following trails into Navajo country. Soon he was trading with the Diné and even accompanying some on hunting trips.

Rather than rein Dodge in, officials in Santa Fe began to seek his assistance, first as a messenger and then as a mediator with Indigenous leaders. That's what brought him to Santa Fe two days after Calhoun's departure in May 1852—Greiner wanted his help calming tensions with the Chiricahua Apache.[50]

Dodge proved so adept at such tasks that Congress soon made it official, appointing him an Indian agent. He became the U.S. point man for the Zuni, Laguna, Acoma and Hopi pueblos, as well as the Navajo Nation.

The Navajo were the largest and most far-flung of New Mexico's Indigenous communities, probably numbering around fourteen thousand in those days.[51] They also had the most land to defend. Settlers called them savages, marauders and worse. Readers of the *Santa Fe Gazette* must have been shocked to learn in June 1853 that Henry Lafayette Dodge—son of a U.S. senator and brother to Augustus Caesar—had decided to live among such wild Indians:

> *Mr. Henry L. Dodge the newly appointed agent for the Navajos is also here, he will remove immediately into the Navajo country and make a permanent settlement, and will reside entirely with the Indians.*
>
> *Mr. Dodge has already formed an extensive acquaintance with the Navajos and will, we doubt not, be able to exercise a salutary influence over them; we regard his appointment as one of the best that could have been made for those Indians.*
>
> *These appointments should be conferred upon such men as Mr. Dodge, who are willing to discharge their duty even at the sacrifice of a comfortable residence among friends.*[52]

The way Dodge saw it, he was among friends. He enjoyed the company of the Diné—if anything, a bit too much. He was forever missing official appointments, and he seemed philosophically opposed to writing reports. He didn't care about decorum or protocol. His financial ledgers were a mess. And yet, as the editors in Santa Fe observed, he was the perfect man for the job.

Dodge spent weeks in the saddle, venturing to places no American knew. He was probably the first American to traverse the length of Canyon de Chelly, invited as a guest. He brought his hosts tools and clothing, sometimes dipping into his own paycheck to purchase them pants, gloves or even a red flannel shirt, like the ones he favored.

He became especially close to Armijo, the Diné leader who'd left Greiner speechless by asking, "Is it American justice that we must give up everything, and receive nothing?" Armijo and Dodge often sat and smoked. They hunted together, too, sometimes setting off for days at a time.

Dodge even managed to win the confidence of Manuelito. Tall, confident and bearing the scars of many battles, Manuelito had every reason to mistrust the Americans. A headman of the Folded Arms People clan, he was married to a daughter of the slain Diné leader Narbona. Manuelito was there the day his father-in-law was cut down by Colonel Washington's troops and scalped by a New Mexican volunteer. And yet, just five years later, Manuelito rode calmly into Santa Fe's central plaza with Dodge and five hundred Churro sheep—a gift to territorial officials, Dodge explained, meant to compensate for some sheep recently stolen by Diné raiders in Algodones.[53] Manuelito had pulled from his own flocks as a gesture of goodwill.

Dodge took a special interest in Diné smiths. Six months after establishing his agency, he hired an American blacksmith and a Mexican silversmith and encouraged the Navajo to watch them work. Given enough time, Dodge was sure that he could earn the trust of the people. He was ready to stake his life on it:

> *Upon my arrival here the Indians expressed much surprise that I should come so far into their country to live, with so small a force. I answered them by exhibiting my Commission from the President with the great seal of United States affixed, appointing me as their agent, and had the interpreter to tell them, that I was commanded by the Governor of the Territory and the President of the United States, to have the same care for them as if they were my relatives and friends, and that I had not the least fear of them, whatever as my intentions were good in every way possible, and to keep them at peace with all nations; that they might kill me whenever they found I gave them bad advice or was an injury to them or their country.[54]*

Delgadito reportedly stopped by Dodge's agency once or twice to observe the colonial smiths at work.[55] If the two men made an impression on each other, we have no record of it. Then again, Dodge probably wouldn't have bothered to write a report. Their next encounter would be much harder to forget.

In June 1855, Governor David Meriwether announced that the time had come for the Navajo to sign another treaty. Meriwether wanted to establish boundaries between the Diné and the settlers—the first formal U.S. effort to limit the Navajo's range. Compared to later treaties, it would be relatively generous, lacking any western border. Meriwether proposed talks in Santa Fe, but Dodge insisted that the governor should meet the Navajo on their own ground. They agreed on a lakeside council at Laguna Negra.[56]

On July 13, Meriwether arrived to find more than two thousand Navajo warriors in attendance.[57] Unlike the reception Colonel Washington received, there were hardly any women or children present—the Diné had learned how dangerous American peace summits could be.

Dodge's friend Armijo was among the headmen present. So were Manuelito and Delgadito—the latter now a headman himself and none too happy with the meeting Dodge had arranged.

Backed by several warriors, Delgadito launched into a fiery denunciation of the Americans. There's no record of what he said, but his grievances are not hard to guess. For all of Dodge's efforts, the Americans had neither stopped the slave raids nor returned any captives. Now they wanted to draw imaginary lines across the earth to corral the Diné like sheep?

Manuelito moved to restore order, ushering Delgadito and his followers from the ramada so the council could continue.[58] But Delgadito wasn't done yet. Meriwether's personal secretary during the talks, William Watts Hart Davis, recalled:

> When we returned to our camp we found it surrounded by hundreds of Indians, and some dozen or more greasy fellows were occupying our tent, and smoking in a manner ridiculously cool and independent, but they soon made tracks after our arrival. The sergeant of the guard attempted to drive them out before our return, when one fellow drew an arrow upon him, but, sooner than have a collision, he had allowed them to remain in quiet possession of the tent.[59]

The rest of the council went just as Dodge had hoped. After Delgadito left, the remaining headmen agreed to sign Meriwether's treaty. Manuelito even accepted from Meriwether a symbolic cane and medal, intended to signify his status as the "principal chief."[60] It was a ridiculous concept—one person speaking on behalf of all the Diné—but Manuelito and the others played along for the sake of peace.

For once, Dodge didn't have to be asked to file a report. He closed 1855 on a bright and hopeful note:

> It is a source of great satisfaction to me to be able to state in this my annual report that the condition of the Navajo tribe of Indians during this year and at present is prosperous in a degree heretofore unknown to them. They are in the full enjoyment of peace with all of its blessings and have raised fine crops of corn, wheat, and vegetables their flocks and herds are rapidly on the increase [which] furnished them with the means of supporting their families with all the absolute necessaries of life in food and raiment....

> *This tribe of Indians manufacture a great variety of woolen goods and of a more substantial kind than any other people in this Territory and their horses and sheep are esteemed the best raised in New Mexico. The late treaty made with them by you if confirmed by the Senate of the U.S. will secure to them a home and country free from the inroads of the New Mexicans which has been from time immemorial one of the causes of difficulty between them.*[61]

Out of habit, U.S. officials did not invite women to participate in the treaty talks of 1855. Yet some began to recognize that Diné women held a commanding position in their communities. It presented a striking contrast to life back in the States, where women were still more than half a century away from winning the right to vote. After returning from Navajo country in 1855, Davis wrote:

> *The modern doctrine of "Woman's Rights" may be said to prevail upon them to a very liberal extent. The women are the real owners of all the sheep, and the men dare not dispose of them without their permission; nor do the husbands make an important bargain without consulting their wives. They admit women into their councils, who sometimes control their deliberations; and they also eat with them.*[62]

The treaty of 1855, like most the United States made with the Diné, was never approved by Congress. Settlers and senators complained that it left too much land to the Navajo. Nevertheless, Dodge worked through the spring and summer to show Armijo, Manuelito and the other headmen progress.

Dodge urged the military to intercept Ute slave raiders from the north. He petitioned Meriwether for materials to equip four flour mills. He ordered more blacksmithing tools and one thousand pounds of iron, reporting that the Diné now counted eighteen smiths among them.

Even Delgadito seemed to warm to the Americans. Major Henry Kendrick, a top field commander who'd become friends with Dodge and supported the peace-building efforts, reported to General John Garland in February 1856, "On our way to Bear Spring we met with Delgadito, the Chief that the General will remember made himself conspicuous at the Treaty of Laguna Negra in July last. He now proclaims himself friendly and there seems a reasonable prospect of him remaining so for the present."[63]

There's no guarantee that Dodge could have prevented all-out war. All that is certain is that the last, best hope for peace died with him in the winter of 1856.

Dodge set out that November with Major Kendrick, a detail of twenty-five soldiers and several Diné scouts, hoping to catch the trail of a group of Chiricahua and White Mountain Apache raiders preying on Zuni and Diné shepherds. Dodge's friend Armijo joined the effort.

After three days in the saddle, and seeing no sign of the Apache, Dodge and Armijo peeled away from the group to hunt for elk. Armijo returned a short time later with his kill, but Dodge never came back. Armijo and the others combed the area for days. They set fires to draw his attention. Nothing. They found some tracks in the snow but couldn't make sense of them. Some wondered if the Apache had taken him prisoner. Others doubted it—the Apache seldom took prisoners.

Soldiers searched most of the winter before finally finding Dodge's remains in the woods. It seemed that the Apache had made quick work of him:

> *From all we could see & learn from the tracks etc. we were led to believe that Captain Dodge was waylaid, murdered & scalped & deprived of his clothes at or near the place where the snow was stained with blood; that one of his murderers put on the clothes & shoes of Captain Dodge & that his tracks were mistaken for those of Capt. Dodge & that it is probably that subsequent to Capt. Dodge's death his horse was led or ridden in various directions to render it difficult for anyone who might come in search of him to trail the horse back to where Capt. Dodge was killed.*[64]

Upon hearing the news, soldiers and Navajo "wept like children at the loss they sustained."[65] They had no idea how great the loss would be. Henry Dodge spent more than three years laying the foundation for a lasting peace. It fell apart in less than half that time.

HELL'S GATE

It's hard to say what upset Major William Brooks more: the fact his personal slave had been killed or that he'd been felled by a Navajo arrow. The one thing that everyone agrees on is that in the summer of 1858, Major Brooks led the United States into war over the death of a young Black man named Jim.

"The boy, strange to say, never uttered a word or exclamation," his master recalled, "but attempted to pull the arrow out, in doing which he broke it off near the head."[66] The major dashed off his report on the killing so hurriedly that James L. Collins, New Mexico's latest superintendent of Indian affairs, must have strained to read the handwriting. Still, Brooks's point was clear enough: he was done negotiating. "Capt. Dodge was of great use to us when we had a similar difficulty in 1854, yet I conceive he was of greater use to the Indians," he wrote. "I think the time for talking to and advising them has passed. They feel too self-confident to appreciate any advice that we can give them."[67]

Born in Ohio in 1821, William Thomas Harbaugh Brooks was just sixteen when he was appointed to the U.S. Military Academy at West Point. His academic record was unimpressive—Brooks graduated forty-sixth in a class of fifty-two—but he soon had a chance to distinguish himself in combat, first in the Seminole War in Florida and then in the war against Mexico. The latter is what brought him to the western frontier, to a post that seemed to have been named with a man like him in mind: Fort Defiance.

Established in 1851, Fort Defiance was the most remote of all U.S. garrisons, two hundred miles from Santa Fe but a mere fifteen miles from

Canyon de Chelly. On army maps, it seemed an impressive projection of U.S. power. In person, it didn't even look like a fort. There was no wall, picketed stockade or defensive barriers of any kind. It was as open as any town. The Navajo certainly thought so; they wandered in and out as they pleased. They were less intimidated than intrigued.

Soldiers hated the place. "Hell's Gate," they called it. Defiance was dusty in the summer and muddy in the winter, with nothing to do between bugle calls. One Christmas, the temperature dropped thirty degrees below zero. The closest thing the troops had to entertainment was the occasional court-martial of a fellow soldier.[68]

Thanks to Henry Dodge—who'd enjoyed the full support of the first two commanders of Fort Defiance, Major Electus Backus and Major Henry Kendrick—there'd been little need for military action. Kendrick tried to maintain the momentum following Dodge's death, but he left the territory upon receiving an appointment to teach at West Point. Brooks was appointed to replace him. John Greiner, the former superintendent for Indian affairs, later testified:

> *The Navajos, while Mr. Dodge was their agent and Major Kendrick and Major Backus were in command of the posts in their country, were friendly and peaceable, owing to the prudence and wisdom with which those officers discharged the duties of their stations, and, in my opinion, had they remained, or people of equal prudence, there would have been no hostilities on the part of the Navajos.*[69]

Years later, Brooks himself would concede that he'd inherited a quiet command: "I took command of Fort Defiance in the latter part of November, 1857. Perfectly peaceful relations existed with the Indians, who were in the habit of visiting the post daily."[70]

If anything, Brooks thought the Navajo had become too comfortable. They strolled the fort's grounds, haggled with soldiers and even gambled while there. Still, it wasn't any of those things that finally set Brooks off. It was the cows.

A dry spring in 1858 prompted Manuelito and some of the other Diné to move their livestock closer to the fort, onto grazing lands used by the military. At the same time, they made gestures intended to ease tensions. In April, Captain John Hatch encountered a large force of warriors. Manuelito was there, and so was the elder headman, Zarcillos Largos. They presented Hatch with 117 sheep, which they had said had been stolen by young raiders.[71]

Despite the gesture, it continued to bother Brooks that the Navajo moved their livestock so near the fort. The following month, he ordered a pair of soldiers into the pasture to drive off the cattle. They started to move the animals away when a group of Diné men rode up and drove the cattle back into the field. Manuelito was among them and accompanied the two soldiers back to the fort. Once there, Manuelito made it clear he hadn't come to apologize. "He became, in fact, perfectly defiant," Brooks recalled. Through the fort's interpreter, Manuelito told Brooks, "The water there is mine, not yours, and the same with the grass. Even the ground it grows from belongs to me, not to you. I will not let you have these things."[72]

The dispute was exactly the sort of brushfire Henry Dodge had been so skilled at putting out. But Dodge's replacement as Navajo agent, William R. Harley, wasn't particularly interested in diplomacy or even in the Navajo. The Missourian didn't arrive in the territory until almost a year after Dodge's death. When he finally showed up, he groused that the Navajo expected "to be treated as they were by Capt. Dodge—that is, to sleep and eat with the agent."[73]

With no one in the Indian Service advocating on the Navajo Nation's behalf, there was little to hold Brooks back. After watching Manuelito ride off, the major sent eighty-one soldiers back into the meadow, with orders to kill the entire herd.

When the troops returned to Fort Defiance, they carried with them a steel cane and medal they'd found in the pasture. They were the items Governor Meriwether had given Manuelito three years earlier, in anointing him the "principal chief" during negotiations. Apparently, Brooks wasn't the only one done talking.

Days passed, then weeks. In Brooks's mind, the issue was resolved. Years later, he still couldn't see the connection between his order to kill the Navajo livestock and the subsequent targeting of his personal slave, Jim. As Brooks recalled:

One morning an Indian came into the garrison and offered a blanket for sale. It was remembered afterwards that he seemed to hang around the bake-houses and other places that soldiers would be like to resort to singly. He finally sold his blanket to a camp woman, whose quarters were not far from my own, between my quarters and the well at which we got our water. As the Indian got on his horse, the servant happened to come along, and as he passed, the Indian drew out his bow and arrow, shooting the boy in the back, between the shoulders, mortally wounding him. He died three days after. The Indian put spurs to his horse, and got away before any alarm could be given.[74]

Brooks responded to the killing by issuing the sort of ultimatum normally reserved for U.S. presidents and Congress, demanding that the Navajo surrender the assassin or face war with the United States. He testified:

When a demand was made for the surrender of the murderer of the servant, the chiefs said such was not their custom....They were willing to compromise, as they were in the habit of doing with Mexicans and Pueblo Indians, by paying any agreed upon amount in horses and sheep. This plan was not listened to for a moment. The delivery of the murderer or war was the alternative offered.

The Indians then contended that the murderer had fled beyond the limits of the nation. They pretended they would send for him, and began to ask for time, etc....Everything was done that was possible to bring them to a sense of the enormity of the crime. They finally brought in word they were after and in close pursuit of the murderer, and would bring him in, dead or alive; and sure enough the next day they brought in the body of a man that they had killed, which on examination proved to be that of one of their captives—in reality a Mexican; when this was made known to them, they admitted the fact, and said they had done all they could or would do.

Military commanders are trained to execute policy, not formulate it. Yet in the first decades of U.S. control, critical policy decisions in New Mexico Territory were left to army officers—men who were often incentivized to fight. For ambitious army officers, the years between the Mexican-American War and the Civil War were not enviable times. Frontier postings were hard, even miserable, with few opportunities to distinguish oneself beyond combat. Battlefield laurels were the surest path to promotion. And in the 1850s, the most convincing "enemies" around were Native American.[75]

After a month passed, and Brooks's demand to surrender the killer had not been met, a column of U.S. troops started toward Canyon de Chelly with orders from Colonel Dixon Miles "to fight these Indians wherever found."[76] American forces killed six warriors in that initial foray, while losing two soldiers. They returned to Fort Defiance with six thousand Navajo sheep they'd seized, along with six Navajo women and children.

As officers made plans for further attacks, they continued to operate independently from the territory's civilian government. Meriwether's successor, Governor Abraham Rencher, expressed his dismay in an October 16 letter to Lewis Cass, the U.S. secretary of state:

> *I did not approve of the manner in which we have been precipitated into this war by the independent action of the commander of the post at Fort Defiance. It seemed to me that Major Brooks should have referred the matter to the head of the department before taking such steps as were likely to result in hostilities. If the commanders of separate posts, acting under local or personal excitement, are allowed thus to involve us in war, there would be no end to Indian wars.*[77]

Louis Kennon, an army surgeon stationed at Defiance in the 1850s, also faulted Brooks, later telling a Congressional committee:

> *Previous to the killing of the negro, the post had been under the command of two very able and philanthropic gentlemen, Majors Kendrick and Backus, who kept the Navajos at peace by keeping the Mexicans away from them.*[78]

Like Greiner, Kennon linked the failure of peace efforts with the failure to address the enslavement of Diné women and children. A decade after seizing control of the territory, the Americans had yet to return a single captive or interdict any of the settlers' slaving expeditions. Kennon testified:

> *I think the Navajoes have been the most abused people on the continent....I know of no family which can raise one hundred and fifty dollars but what purchases a Navajo slave, and many families own four or five—the trade in them being as regular as the trade in pigs or sheep.*

Near the end of 1858, as the army pressed ahead with reprisals over the killing of Brooks's slave, Governor Rencher sent a follow-up letter to Secretary of State Cass in Washington, D.C. He confessed uncertainty over what would come next:

> *It is certain that no great advantage has as yet been obtained over the Indians. Their knowledge of the country enables them to keep out of the way of our troops, who at times capture and destroy some of their stock, of which they have a large quantity. The war, in my opinion, was unwisely precipitated upon the Indians, and might have been avoided by prudence and fairness on the part of the Indian agent. The rendition of the murderer of*

the negro boy was improperly made as sine qua non. *In the armistice that is waived, the Indians alleged that the band to which he belonged has left their country and been outlawed by them. The great object now should be to obtain such an arrangement as will secure the settlements against future depredations by the Indians, and to secure the faithful observance of such an arrangement by the Navajos. Whether they have been sufficiently chastised to bring them to these conditions, remains to be seen.*[79]

Governor Rencher would not have to wait long to find out. Around this time, the Diné began using a new word for the Americans: Bilagáana, shortened from Bildá' hxáiijíghání, meaning, "Those we fight against."

ENEMY WAY

I t was no simple business, pulling an arrow out of a man. Dr. Joseph Bill served as the surgeon at Fort Defiance for less than a year, yet in that short time he managed to conduct what remains the definitive study on the subject. In preparing his twenty-two-page paper for the *American Journal of Medical Sciences*, "Notes on Arrow Wounds," the doctor had no shortage of data points:

> An expert bowman can easily discharge six arrows per minute, and a man wounded with one is almost sure to receive several arrows. In the above table, when a man was wounded in more places than one, the most serious wound, or that which immediately caused his death, is recorded. We have not seen more than one or two men wounded by a single arrow only. In three of our soldiers shot by Nabajoes [sic] we counted forty-two arrow wounds; this is an extreme case, as the manufacture of the arrow costs the Indian too much labour and time to expend one unnecessarily.[80]

As Dr. Bill walked his readers through various cases, rattling off the names of army privates picked off on patrol by Diné warriors, he noted that the greatest problem, from a clinical standpoint, was that the arrows hit with enough velocity to penetrate the thickest bones:

> We have seen an arrow shot at a distance of one hundred yards, so deeply imbedded in an oak plank, that it required great force, applied by strong tooth-forceps, to remove it. In the case of a man shot in the shaft of the

humerus by an arrow, it was only after using both knees, applied to the ends of the bone as a counter-extending force, and a stout pair of tooth-forceps, that we succeeded in removing the foreign body.

Unfortunately for most of Dr. Bill's patients, the Navajo had constructed their arrows with just such a scene in mind—the arrowheads were engineered to break off in the body:

Let us suppose a case to illustrate and explain our meaning. An arrow is shot at a man at a distance of fifty yards. It penetrates his abdomen, and without wounding an intestine or a great vessel, lodges in the body of one of the vertebrae. The arrow is grasped by the shaft by some officious friend, and after a little tugging is pulled out. We said the arrow is pulled out. This was a mistake; it is the shaft only of the arrow that is pulled out. The angular and jagged head has been left buried in the bone to kill—for so it surely will—the victim.

What's more, the arrowheads were no longer made of stone. Diné metalsmiths had turned their skills to war:

The head is made of soft hoop iron, filed into the form of an isosceles triangle, and furnished with a stem to attach it to the shaft. This stem is an inch long by one-eighth of an inch broad, and is of one piece with the rest of the head. An arrow-head varies in length from half an inch to two inches, and half an inch to three-quarters of an inch in breadth at its base. No two arrows are alike.

Dr. Bill concluded that injuries by arrow were more lethal than gunshot wounds, particularly considering the generally poor quality of Navajo firearms. Given his unique perspective, he may have been the only man in camp worrying about arrows on that moonless night in 1860, when one thousand Navajo warriors descended on Fort Defiance, their gun muzzles flashing like stars.

Manuelito had been gathering warriors ever since the blowup in 1858. Major Brooks left Navajo country on medical leave later that year, but Manuelito's position did not soften: the Americans should be pushed out, and quickly, before they could solidify their grip on Dinétah.

Not everyone agreed. The elder headmen, Zarcillos Largos, was among those still arguing for restraint. However, the U.S. Army ultimately helped

Barboncito vowed, "I will never leave my country, not even if it means that I will be killed."
National Museum of the American Indian.

bolster Manuelito's case for war with its repeated incursions into Navajo territory and unwillingness to stop the slave trade.

In late 1859—five months before the Navajo attack on Fort Defiance—a government Ute agent in Abiquiú watched more than one hundred Ute and Hispano raiders set out for Navajo country. The agent, Albert Pfeiffer, explained that "he thought it best to let them go, if they wanted to." A few weeks later, the agent reported seeing the slavers return with twenty-three captive children, all but two of them little girls.[81] No effort was made to prevent the kidnappings. Barboncito and Delgadito decided that Manuelito was right: the time had come to fight.

In January 1860, Diné warriors launched a campaign east of the Rio Grande, raiding settlements for livestock and leaving several ranches in flames. In February, they attacked a company of forty-four soldiers guarding cattle grazing at a military hay camp.

American commanders looked at the map of Navajo country and decided that another outpost was needed, this time near Bear Springs. They named it Fort Fauntleroy and pulled Company G of the Third Infantry out of Fort Defiance to occupy it, leaving behind a diminished force of 138 men.

Diné warriors watched as the men of Company G left Fort Defiance and turned their gaze toward the sky, knowing what would come next.

Shortly after 1:00 a.m. on April 30, 1860, the moon dipped below the horizon, casting Fort Defiance in darkness. Lieutenant William Whipple had just conducted an unannounced inspection of the guard. Feeling uneasy for days, Whipple decided to walk the perimeter that night. It was a prescient choice:

> But for his conscientious and thorough attention to his duty that night, and his personal, minute and thoughtful instructions to every man of his guard, our subsequent efforts might have been unavailing. As it was, the enemy was met by such prompt and efficient a resistance by the guard that the garrison had time to turn out and take position. The place was surrounded by hills, and these were alive with Navajoes.[82]

Any man who slept through the first shots awoke to a steady drum roll. Known as the Old Guard, the Third Infantry had rallied to the sound of the "long roll" for nearly a century, all the way back to the War of Independence. Now finding themselves under attack from three sides, the men fell into formation and fanned out under the direction of three officers. One recalled, "As I approached the company quarters, the First

Sergeant gravely saluted, while a shower of balls were pattering upon the log building, and remarked pleasantly, 'They seem to think they can take us this morning, Lieutenant.'"[83]

The next four hours saw combat of every kind. Diné warriors broke through the perimeter, taking cover behind woodpiles and entering a storehouse. The men of the Third held their ground—their lives depended on it. Finally, just before sunrise, Manuelito ordered the warriors to withdraw. By the time there was enough light for the soldiers to use the sights of their rifles and carbines, the Diné were gone.

The Navajo lost seven or eight men that night. Remarkably, the Americans lost just one, a twenty-eight-year-old private named Sylvester Johnson. At first, it appeared that Johnson had been shot, but when Dr. Bill examined the body, he found an arrowhead lodged inside the young man's chest. Someone had knelt beside the wounded soldier and snapped off the arrow's shaft.

American commanders were stunned by the attack. They ordered Fort Defiance abandoned but reversed themselves days later, vowing to muster troops for a counter assault. Settlers were unwilling to wait. They formed vigilante militias, launching private expeditions into Navajo country before the army had time to regroup. The territory's superintendent of Indian affairs, James L. Collins, in his side job as the publisher of the *Santa Fe Gazette*, used the newspaper to encourage the citizen attacks:

> *Brave hearts, animated with the consciousness that they are engaged in the right, that they bear arms in a just cause, that theirs is a work which commends itself to the appropriation of civilized humanity, cannot fail to accomplish the relief of their impoverished country from the raids of a foe that knows no mercy, that has for so many years subsisted upon the fruits of the toil of the industrious citizens of the Territory and that has been a vagabond upon the face of the earth.*
>
> *This is an object which must be accomplished before our people can with security lie down when the shades of night surround them; this must be done before our people can with certainty say, their flocks and their herds are their own; it must be done before our people can be released from the thraldom of servitude to the barbarian. And the volunteer force that is about to go into the field are the ones to do it. Never did any army go forth in a more righteous cause; never did one go forth in pursuit of a more devilish enemy.*[84]

So began what the Diné call "The Fearing Time," an eight-year odyssey during which the entire Navajo Nation was either hunted or held in captivity—and not just by the army and private militias. The slave trade that began under Spain, and expanded under Mexico, exploded in the chaos of the American-led war.

Based on an analysis of baptismal records, the anthropologist David M. Brugge calculated that at least 2,457 Navajo were captured and enslaved during the 1860s, most of them children.[85] When one considers the population of the nation was probably around 14,000, it seems that hardly a family escaped untouched.

Following the Navajo attack on Fort Defiance, U.S. troops altered their own rules of engagement, adopting tactics similar to those of slave raiders. American soldiers executed Diné men on the spot, took women and children captive and seized whatever livestock they found.

U.S. Major Henry H. Sibley—second in command of the American forces under Colonel Edward Canby—led retaliatory operations in the area of Canyon de Chelly that fall. On October 14, he reported, "During the night an Indian spy was wounded by one of the pickets, trailed and brought into camp next morning. After eliciting from him all information possible he was shot by my order."[86]

Just over a week later, Sibley's scouts spotted a large herd of Navajo horses near Black Mesa. They turned out to be Delgadito's; he'd established a temporary camp there. On October 23, Sibley's forces attacked:

2 companies of Rifles were dispatched to the right to secure the herd in view, to gather up any flocks they might encounter and to destroy any opposing enemy, whilst the 2 Companies were held in reserve to cooperate with them or to cut off any flying parties. The distance to the herd of horses and to the Indian camp was so great that the flocks were all secured and the Indians dispersed, destroyed or captured before the 2 reserve Companies could reach the ground. The herds amounting in the aggregate to 200 horses and 2000 sheep. The number of Indians reported killed 5, prisoners 3 women & 2 children—all of Delgadito's band, one of the wealthiest of the nation.

In early November, Sibley reported executing another prisoner:

At night a brother of the celebrated chief Gordo was wounded by one of the Cavalry pickets, trailed by his blood next morning, found, brought into camp, and was shot by the order of the Commander of the Column.

With Sibley now holding five of his band prisoner, Delgadito rode into the American headquarters that winter under a white flag of protection. He told Colonel Canby that he and some of the other headmen were ready to negotiate. The morale of the Navajo had suffered another heavy blow a few weeks earlier, when news spread that the elder headman Zarcillos Largos had been killed. Canby rejected Delgadito's peace overture, telling him the United States would accept nothing less than unconditional surrender. Delgadito rode off to deliver the news.[87]

Before the Civil War, Confederate general Henry Sibley commanded U.S. troops in New Mexico, where he ordered the execution of Navajo prisoners. *Library of Congress.*

A few weeks later, Canby announced that he'd had a change of heart. He sent word that he would meet with Delgadito and the others to negotiate a new treaty. The reason for the turnabout isn't hard to guess: the army now had bigger worries than the Navajo. The debate over slavery had devolved into talk of southern secession. Five days before Christmas, South Carolina declared that it had left the Union. A headline in the *Charleston Mercury* proclaimed, "The tea has been thrown overboard, the revolution of 1860 has been initiated."

After some back and forth, Canby presented a new treaty to the Navajo on February 18, 1861. Delgadito and twenty-three other headmen signed it, the largest number ever to make their mark on a treaty. They agreed to all of Canby's terms, making no demands of their own. Canby expressed hope that the two nations had secured "an absolute and permanent peace."[88] One month after signing the treaty, he wrote:

> *I have the honor to report that the Navajo chiefs appear to be carrying out in good faith the conditions of the treaty, and I have no doubt of the permanent settlement of these troubles if the inroads of Mexicans can be restrained.*
>
> *The Navajos report today another inroad by the Mexicans near the north-eastern extremity of the Tunicha Mountains in which the people of 15 rancherias were killed or carried off. The Navajos involved in this raid are of the families of Herrero Grande, Vicente Baca and El Chapador, and it has happened unfortunately for our influence with these people that in this*

and the instance already reported, many of the Navajoes belonging to these
families were absent for the purpose of recovering stolen property.[89]

The Navajo abided by the treaty despite the slave raids. They continued
to do so even after the Americans turned on one another. In April 1861—a
year after the Navajo attack on Fort Defiance—units of the newly organized
Confederate States Army staged their own predawn assault on Fort Sumter,
South Carolina.

Within weeks, nearly half of the Regular Army officers in New Mexico
had resigned their commissions to join the rebels. Major Henry Sibley—
Canby's second in command and the officer who had attacked Delgadito's
band the previous November—rode east across the Rio Grande with plans
to mount an invasion of his own.

Born in Louisiana and raised in Missouri, Sibley received an appointment
to the U.S. Military Academy at age seventeen. While serving on the
frontier in the 1850s, he developed a packable tent and stove kit capable of
sheltering up to twelve men. It would be a stretch to say Sibley "invented"
the setup, which mimicked the design of Comanche lodges of the era.
He was, however, the first person to think of patenting it. Under an 1858
agreement with the War Department, Sibley was promised five dollars for
every tent made. But when he turned his back on the U.S. government,
he turned his back on any royalties from the U.S. Patent Office, and
never received a penny for the nearly forty-four thousand "Sibley tents"
manufactured during the war.[90]

When Sibley left New Mexico for Texas, he had a much larger prize in
mind. In a Confederate reimagining of Manifest Destiny, he planned to
return with an army that would wrest control of the territory from the Union
and punch through to California, extending slavery all the way to the Pacific.

The plan was not that far-fetched. At the onset of war, U.S. commanders
shifted forces out of New Mexico to reinforce positions farther east. The
moves left them vulnerable to invasion.

To fill the void, Union army commanders turned to volunteers from the
local settlements. The government offered a $100 "bounty" for enlisting,
on top of $13 per month. By the end of 1861, 3,500 volunteers were in
active service in New Mexico, in addition to numerous independent militias
formed by settlers.[91]

One New Mexican officer quickly rose to favor—Manuel Chaves, the
Little Lion of Cebolleta, scion of New Mexico's most celebrated slaving
family. Now forty-three years old, Chaves was idolized by his fellow

militiamen. Over the years, he'd led many of them on raids against the Navajo. Now faced with an invasion of Texans, the settlers joined together to form the Second New Mexico Volunteers and elected Chaves as their lieutenant colonel.

Aware of Chaves's popularity and years of experience, the army awarded him command of Fort Fauntleroy, the new outpost not far from Bear Springs—the same watering hole where the Little Lion had nursed his wounds all those years before, after losing a brother to Navajo arrows.

It was an unusual move, giving so much authority to an officer from a volunteer regiment. Once again, the Americans would realize their mistake too late.

ON THE OCCASION REFERRED TO ABOVE

Department of New Mexico,
Assistant Adjutant General's Office
July 26, 1865

Captain: It is understood that you were at Fort Fauntleroy several years since, when some Navajoes were fired upon by order of a Lieutenant Colonel Chaves.

If you were present on the occasion referred to above, the general commanding desires that you make by return mail a detailed account of the whole affair as you remember it. Great care should be taken to have it exact, as it is to be laid before the Congressional Committee on Indian Affairs. Respectfully, your obedient servant,

Ben C. Cutler,
Assistant Adjutant General

———————————

Fort Wingate,
New Mexico
September 7, 1865

Major: In compliance with instructions received from Headquarters, Department of New Mexico, assistant adjutant general's office, Santa

Fe, New Mexico, dated July 26, 1865, I have the honor to make the following statement:

Sometime during the month of September, 1861, as near as I can recollect, horse-racing was frequent at Fort Fauntleroy, New Mexico, and high bets made by officers and Navajo Indians at the post. Government stock was staked by the officers as if it were their own. If lost, all right; and if won, so much gained by them by means of government property. I was not an eye-witness of the staking of government property, but proof can be furnished.

The Navajo Indians appeared to be at that time very friendly to the government; they visited the post by hundreds every day, and were rationed on meat and flour. This friendly feeling of the Navajoes was kept up until the time of the horse-races. There were three different races, the third race in order to give the Indians satisfaction. Large bets, larger than on either of the other races, were made on both sides. The Indians flocked in by hundreds, women and children; some of them mounted on fine ponies, richly dressed, and all appeared to be there to see the race, and not with any hostile intentions.

The troops in the post had orders to be under arms, but that they might go to the gate to see the race. About noon the race came off. Lieutenant Ortiz rode Dr. Kavanaugh's horse. The Indian's horse did not run a hundred yards before it ran off the track. I being at the upper end of the track, could not see the cause of it, but the report was that the Indian's bridle broke.[92] The Indians then said the race was not fair, and that the bets should be drawn; the opposite party, not satisfied with the proposition, would not give up what they had won, and consequently the commanding officer gave orders to the officer of the day not to allow the Navajoes inside of the post. The horse was taken inside the post, followed by the whole winning party, the drums beating, fifes and fiddles screeching, etc., etc. So the procession went whooping and hallooing to receive the part they had won. Finally, whilst thus occupied a shot was fired at or near the post. Every man then ran to arm himself. Companies did not regularly form, but every man ran wherever he thought fit. The shot was fired on account of Private Morales, sentinel No. 2, whilst opposing an Indian's entrance to the post. It was said that the Indian was intoxicated and tried to force his entrance past the sentinel. At that instant the shot was fired and the Indian fell. Who fired is not known. As soon as this was ascertained, the Navajoes, squaws and children, ran in all directions and were shot and bayoneted. I tried my best to form the company I was first sergeant of, and succeeded in forming about twenty men—it being very hard work. I then marched out to the east side of the post; there I saw a soldier murdering two little children and a woman. I hallooed immediately to the soldier to stop. He looked up, but did not obey my order. I ran up as quick as I could, but could not get there soon enough to prevent him from killing the two innocent children and wounding severely the squaw. I ordered his belts to be taken off and taken prisoner to the post. On my arrival in the post I met Lieutenant Ortiz with a pistol at full cock, saying, "Give back this soldier his arms, or else I'll shoot you, God damn you," which circumstances I reported to my company commander, he reporting the same to the colonel commanding, and the answer he received from the colonel was, "that Lieutenant Ortiz did perfectly right, and that he gave credit to the soldier who murdered the children and wounded the squaw." Meantime the colonel had given orders to the officer of the day to have the artillery (mountain howitzers) brought out and to open upon the Indians. The sergeant in charge of the mountain howitzers pretended not to understand the order given, for he considered it as an unlawful order; but being cursed by the officer of the day, and threatened, he had to execute the order or else get himself in trouble. The Indians scattered all over the valley below the post, attacked the post herd, wounded the Mexican herder, but did not succeed in getting any stock; also attacked the expressman some ten miles from the post, took his horse and mailbag and wounded him in the arm. After the massacre there were no more Indians to be seen about the post with the exception of a few squaws, favorites of the officers. The commanding officer endeavored to make peace again with the Navajoes by sending some of the favorite squaws to talk with the chiefs; but the only satisfaction the squaws received was a good flogging. An expressman was sent shortly after the affairs above mentioned happened, but private letters were not allowed to be sent, and letters that reached the post office at Fauntleroy were found opened but not forwarded. To the best of my knowledge the number of Navajoes killed was twelve or fifteen; the number wounded could not be ascertained. There were only two wounded bucks and one wounded squaw in the hospital. The rest wounded must have been taken away by the tribe.

I am, sir, very respectfully, your obedient servant,

NICHOLAS HODT,
Captain, 1st Cavalry, New Mexico Volunteers[93]

PART II

BEAUTY BEHIND

THE PALACE OF THE GOVERNORS

No one recalls if they were running toward something or away from it, but sometime in the eleventh century, James Henry Carleton's maternal ancestors left Italy and never looked back. They settled first in Germany and then England, before finally landing in the Americas around 1630. Somewhere along the way, they adopted the optimistic family motto, "He who transplanted, well settled."[94]

Abigail Phelps Carleton must have imagined herself well settled in 1814, the year she became pregnant with her first child. Her husband, John, boasted American roots as deep as hers. His family had arrived in 1638 on the ship that delivered the colonies' first printing press.

Their home sat on the easternmost tip of the United States: Eastport, Maine, on tiny Moose Island. As she made plans for the baby, Abigail might have read newspaper accounts of the latest war with England. The conflict must have seemed a far-off affair. Merchants and residents in Maine had been cool toward the war from its start in 1812. They saw the English as natural trading partners and viewed themselves as neutral bystanders. Even the U.S. soldiers stationed on Moose Island considered themselves on sojourn from the war, right up until the July afternoon in 1814 when several English warships pulled into view, carrying an invasion force so large that it boasted more musicians than the Americans had officers.[95]

Captain Jacob Varnum, who surrendered along with the rest of the garrison at Fort Sullivan, wrote in his journal, "When we were sitting in our piazza on the morning, enjoying a cool breeze from the ocean, suddenly the reach or strait inside of Grand Manan became whitened by the canvas of a large fleet of vessels making directly for our harbor. It was a beautiful sight but rather ominous."[96]

Abigail Carleton and her husband, John, fled with other residents just across the channel, to the town of Lubec. Abigail gave birth five months after Moose Island fell, and for the first few years of his life, her son could look across the water and see the flag of an occupying army.

Growing up, James Carleton did not envision a military career for himself, far from it. Once upon a time, the man who would be remembered for waging war on Native Americans wanted to write novels about them—sagas of Indigenous America, in the style of James Fenimore Cooper. In his early twenties, Carleton sought career advice from another writer, one only a few years older than himself but wildly successful, both in America and his native England. Remarkably, Charles Dickens wrote back:

> *I am not, of course, so good a judge as you should be of the degree of encouragement which America affords her own citizens. At the same time I cannot but think that good tales—especially such as you describe, connected with the customs and history of America's aboriginal inhabitants who every day become more interesting as their numbers diminish—would surely find patrons and readers in her great cities.*[97]

By the time Dickens's letter had reached Maine, Carleton had already answered another call, this one from Governor John Fairfield. The English were once again threatening invasion, and able-bodied men were needed to defend Maine's northern border. Carleton enlisted in the summer of 1838. He was commissioned as a first lieutenant in a volunteer militia and would rarely be seen out of uniform again.

When tensions eased on the border and his volunteer militia disbanded, Carleton promptly enlisted in the Regular Army. He set his sights on the cavalry and the western frontier. His service took him to Kansas and then Nebraska and Missouri. Along America's tense southern borders, he got his first glimpse of Mexico and the Lone Star Republic of Texas. He picked up a wife along the way, too: Sophia Garland Wolfe, the niece of U.S. General John Garland.

Carleton encountered many Native Americans in his travels, including the Comanche, "Lords of the Plains" and sworn enemies of the Texans. It was the stuff of good tales, just as Dickens had suggested. In 1844 and 1845,

Carleton submitted several anonymous "Prairie Log Books" to a New York magazine. In them, he offered readers an idyllic view of frontier life:

> *In garrison the scene is ever the same but talk to a soldier of a campaign, picture to him the broad plains and magnificent mountains, the groves and the rivers: he will fire up in a moment and his heart will pant with impatience to mount and be away again. He will recall the staunch and cheerful comrades; the roasted buffalo ribs, the broiled venison and the coffee; then, too, the sociable pipe and the accompanying story, the joke and song.*[98]

In the South, Carleton got his first close look at slavery. Whatever qualms other New Englanders had about the "peculiar institution," Carleton embraced it. He purchased two Black slaves—a man and a woman—in Missouri and took them to New Mexico when his unit was deployed there in 1851.

Carleton and his wife held the pair at their home in Santa Fe until the following year, when records show he sold them to the territory's newly appointed governor, William Carr Lane. With no law allowing slavery in New Mexico, they justified the sale as an effort to secure "good and humane masters" and included this description of the captives in the sales receipt:

> *One Negro Man named Benjamin, a slave for life, who is about twenty-one years of age, being the same slave which the said James Henry Carleton bought of George Stille of Missouri.*
>
> *One Negro Woman named Hannah, a slave for life, who is about twenty-eight years of age, and who is the same slave which the said James Henry Carleton bought of Mathew Hughes of Missouri.*
>
> *To have and to hold each of the above mentioned slaves with all the right thereunto belonging to the said William Carr Lane, to his successors and assigns, In Trust, to and for the several uses, intents, and purposes, hereinafter mentioned, namely:*
>
> *First: That he shall hire out said slaves at his discretion.*
>
> *Second: That he shall sell said slaves to the best advantage and shall apply the proceeds of said sale to the payment of the debts aforesaid and the interest due thereon, and the surplus, if any may remain from the hire and sale of said slaves, if any there be, as just expressed, after discharging the expenses of this trust, the said party of the second part, shall pay over to the wife of said party of the first part, and in case of her death, to the legal representative of the children of said James Henry Carleton.*

General James H. Carleton, architect of
the Long Walk of the Navajo, became
convinced that their land held vast
deposits of gold. *Library of Congress.*

*And it is hereby covenanted and agreed between said parties that Private
sales may be made of said slaves, so that good and humane masters may
be secured for them and the said party of the second part shall not in any
manner be accountable if the said slaves shall die or run away.*[99]

Maybe Carleton sold his slaves out of moral misgivings. Maybe it was
a way to curry favor with the new governor of the territory. Or maybe it
was just the expedient thing for an ambitious army officer to do, lest an
opportunity arise in one of America's resolutely free states. Eventually, one
did, and it set Carleton on a collision course with the Navajo Nation by way
of the California Gold Rush.

When the Civil War began, Union army recruiters found themselves in
desperate need of men. The gold fields of California were teeming with
men—most of them young, mobile and used to roughing it. The War
Department tapped Carleton to recruit, train and lead 1,500 of those miners
against the Confederacy.

In February 1862, when Henry Sibley followed through with his invasion
of New Mexico, Carleton and the California First Infantry marched east
to meet him. Dubbed the California Column, the volunteers trekked across
nine hundred miles of mountain and desert, skirmishing with Apache

fighters along the way. They also managed to look for gold. One volunteer claimed that they'd prospected the entire route to Tucson.[100]

Sibley and the Texans briefly managed to take New Mexico, supported by secessionists who splintered off to form a Confederate territory, which they named Arizona. Finding Fort Defiance abandoned, the rebels burned it to the ground and claimed Santa Fe for the South. They didn't stay long. In June, a Union army expressman named John Jones outraced Apache warriors to deliver the news: "The column from California is really coming." As Union troops staged counter-offenses and the California Column drew near, Sibley's forces withdrew back into Texas.

And so, three hundred years after the conquistadors first came looking for treasure, James H. Carleton landed in Santa Fe with an army of gold miners.

Awarded the brevet rank of brigadier general, Carleton replaced Edward Canby as commander of the Department of New Mexico in September 1862. His headquarters were located at the Palace of the Governors, a grand name for a modest complex of low-slung adobe buildings in the heart of Santa Fe. It is colonial America's oldest structure and arguably its most storied, first established by Spain around 1610. Following the Pueblo Revolt of 1680, the palace briefly became home to dozens of Native families. Then the conquistadors returned, still dreaming of gold and glory. Over the centuries, it served as the seat of power for three successive colonial administrations—four if you count the Confederates. One of Carleton's first acts was to reissue Canby's order establishing martial law in the territory, preserving sweeping authority for the military and, of course, himself.

Sitting by the fireplace in the governor's office, far from the battlefields of Shiloh and Antietam, Carleton began to think that maybe the Spaniards were right all along. In spite of all evidence to the contrary, and three centuries of cautionary tales, he became convinced that Navajo land held vast deposits of gold. He wrote to his superiors in Washington, promising an enormous payoff if they'd back his plans for the territory:

> *There is no doubt in my mind that one of the richest gold countries in the world is along the affluent to the Gila, which enter it from the north along its whole course. Thus you can see one reason why the rebels want, and why we may not permit them ever to have, a country evidently teeming with millions on millions of wealth....If I only had one more good regiment of California infantry, composed, as that infantry is, of practical miners, I would place it in the Gila country. While it would exterminate the Indians, who are a scourge to New Mexico, it would protect people who might wish*

to go there to open up the country, and would virtually be a military colony when the war ended, whose interests would lead the officers and soldiers to remain in the new El Dorado.[101]

"Exterminate the Indians." Even as he wrote it, Carleton knew that it wasn't possible. In other letters, he acknowledged that the American public would not stand for an overt war of annihilation. A reservation was needed, someplace to move the tribe, clearing the way for his imagined mining colony.

Carleton wasted no time weighing alternate sites; he was sure he knew the perfect place. About 165 miles east-southeast of Santa Fe—and nearly four hundred miles east of Canyon de Chelly—he'd once seen a stand of cottonwoods growing hard on the Pecos River. Bosque Redondo, the Spanish explorers named it, "the round forest." Only someone who'd crossed a desert would think to call it that. The ground was hard, dry and studded with mesquite. The river water was so alkaline that animals sometimes refused to drink from it. "When bad men die," the Texas buffalo hunters used to say, "they either go to hell or the Pecos."[102]

Carleton set aside forty square miles. From his perspective, the site offered unique advantages, placing the Navajo between the settlers of the Rio Grande Valley and Comanche warriors riding in from the Plains. One Indigenous nation could be used as a buffer against another.

With enough hard work, Carleton was sure that the reservation could be turned into a prosperous farming community, easily capable of supporting the entire Navajo Nation, which the general confidently estimated at five thousand. Carleton always sounded sure of himself, even when he was wrong.

The general offered varying justifications for exiling the Diné, depending on his audience. When addressing his superiors in Washington, he emphasized the potential windfall in gold and other minerals. To the settlers of New Mexico, he presented it as a protective police action, designed to bring peace to the region. In an open letter to the *Santa Fe Gazette*, Carleton wrote:

When I came here this time it not only became my professional business, but my duty to the residents and to the Government, to devise some plan which might, with God's blessing, forever bring these troubles to an end.

Soon after my arrival, eighteen Navajo chiefs came to see me to request a peace treaty. I told them it was not necessary to go through the form of treaty making; that if their people committed no murders, there would be peace without a treaty. Hereafter, I would judge their sincerity by their acts.

The Indians were told that if they were guilty of further depredations, they would be punished, as sure as the sun shone down upon them. It would be a war which they would long remember. In reply the Indians said they had never before been refused a treaty, and promised to try to keep their people from making trouble.[103]

When Carleton met with eighteen Diné headmen in December 1862—Delgadito and Barboncito among them—he was not forthcoming. He assured them that peace was still possible; he did not tell them that preparations for their exile were already underway.

Two months earlier, Carleton ordered the establishment of Fort Sumner and the Bosque Redondo reservation. The first three companies of infantry arrived on site in November. More ominously, he'd already launched a campaign against the Mescalero Apache people to the east.

The Mescalero Apache numbered in the hundreds back then; they hardly needed a reservation the size of Bosque Redondo. But their relocation offered a small-scale run-up to Carleton's plan for exiling the Navajo. In his October 12 order declaring war on the Mescalero, Carleton wrote:

All Indian men of that tribe are to be killed whenever and wherever you can find them. The women and children will not be harmed, but you will take them prisoners, and feed them at Fort Stanton until you receive other instructions about them. If the Indians send in a flag and desire to treat for peace, say to the bearer that when the people of New Mexico were attacked by the Texans, the Mescaleros broke their treaty of peace, and murdered innocent people, and ran off their stock; that now our hands are untied, and you have been sent to punish them for their treachery and their crimes; that you have no power to make peace; that you are there to kill them wherever you can find them; that if they beg for peace, their chiefs and twenty of their principal men must come to Santa Fe to have a talk here; but tell them fairly and frankly that you will keep after their people and slay them until you receive orders to desist from these headquarters; that this making of treaties for them to break whenever they have an interest in breaking them will not be done any more; that that time has passed by; that we have no faith in their promises; that we believe if we kill some of their men in fair, open war, they will be apt to remember that it will be better for them to remain at peace than to be at war. I trust that this severity, in the long run, will be the most humane course that could be pursued toward these Indians.[104]

As word of the campaign against the Mescalero spread, Diné leaders received more troubling news. The Americans were establishing two new forts in Navajo country. One, named Fort Wingate, was sited among the fertile pastures of the Ojo de Gallo Valley. The other, built over the charred remains of Fort Defiance, was named Fort Canby in honor of Carleton's predecessor. "Built" might be an overstatement. In December 1862, Captain Julius Shaw wrote from Fort Wingate:

The fort looks vastly fine on paper, but as yet it has no other existence. The garrison consists of four companies of my regiment—the Fourth New Mexico Mounted Rifles—and we live in, or rather exist, in holes or excavations, made in the earth, over which our cloth tents are pitched. We are supplied with fire places, chimneys, etc. and on the whole, during the beautiful, pleasant weather of the past few weeks, have enjoyed ourselves quite well. Our camp presents the appearance of a gypsy encampment more than anything else I can compare it to.[105]

The Diné headmen could not understand Carleton's drive toward war or his refusal to talk peace. After all, they'd held tight to the terms of the 1861 treaty with Canby, even after the massacre at Fort Fauntleroy. They abided by the treaty even when the Bilagáana turned on one another and the graycoats attacked from the east. As the historian David M. Brugge observed:

There's no solid evidence that Navajos took advantage of the Confederate invasion of New Mexico to raid and plunder at will. Indeed, the reverse seems to be the case. The New Mexicans took advantage of the situation to raid the Navajos in greater numbers. The Navajos tried, with little success, to continue the peace established by Canby's treaty.[106]

In April 1863, Carleton finally revealed his plans to the Navajo. By that time, the campaign against the Mescalero was winding down; more than four hundred had been sent to Bosque Redondo. Meeting with Barboncito and Delgadito near Cubero, Carleton told the brothers that their people now faced the same choice as the Mescalero Apache: Go to the reservation called Bosque Redondo…or die.

"I will not go to the Bosque," Barboncito told Carleton. "I will never leave my country, not even if it means that I will be killed."[107] Carleton let Barboncito and Delgadito return to their people, wanting word of his ultimatum to spread. He already had everything he needed: a far-off reservation, authorization to forcibly remove the Navajo and troops who were itching for a fight. The volunteers of the First New Mexico Cavalry even honored Carleton with a campaign marching song:

Here's a health to Gen'l Carleton, that wise and brave hero
His arrival was a blessing great, to speed New Mexico;
May he win unfading laurels and sorrow never know
And live to see the country free from Johnny Navajo.

Johnny Navajo—O Johnny Navajo!
We'll first chastise, then civilize, bold Johnny Navajo![108]

On June 14, 1863, Carleton sent a private letter to Army General in Chief Henry Halleck, promising "a country as rich if not richer in mineral wealth than California."[109] The following day, he issued General Orders No. 15, authorizing the famous frontiersman Christopher "Kit" Carson to launch a campaign against the Navajo:

For a long time past the Navajoe Indians have murdered and robbed the people of New Mexico. Last winter when eighteen of their chiefs came to Santa Fe to have a talk, they were warned—and were told to inform their people—that for these murders and robberies the tribe must be punished, unless some binding guarantees should be given that in [the] future these outrages should cease. No such guarantees have yet been given. But on the contrary, additional murders, and additional robberies have been perpetrated upon the persons and property of unoffending citizens. It is therefore ordered that Colonel Christopher Carson, with a proper military force, proceed without delay to a point in the Navajoe country known as Pueblo Colorado, and there establish a defensible Depot for his supplies and Hospital; and thence to prosecute a vigorous war upon the men of this tribe until it is considered at these Head Quarters that they have been effectually punished for their long continued atrocities.[110]

In Carleton's June 23 instructions to Carson, he reiterated his ultimatum to Delgadito and Barboncito:

Send for Delgadito and Barboncito again and repeat what I before told them, and tell them that I shall feel very sorry if they refuse to come in; that we have no desire to make war upon them and other good Navajoes; but the troops cannot tell the good from the bad, and we neither can nor will tolerate their staying as a peace party among those against whom we intend to make war. Tell them they can have until the twentieth day of July of this year to come in—they and all those who belong to what they call the peace party; that after that day every Navajo that is seen will be considered as hostile and treated accordingly; that after that day the door now open will be closed. Tell them to say all this to their people, and that as sure as that the sun shines all this will come true.

I am, colonel, respectfully, your obedient servant,
JAMES H. CARLETON,
Brigadier General, Commanding[111]

SIFTING OUT THE HEARTS OF MEN

Mine eyes have seen the glory of the coming of the Lord
He is trampling out the vintage where the grapes of wrath are stored
He hath loosed the fateful lightning of His terrible swift sword
His truth is marching on.
—"The Battle Hymn of the Republic"

By the time the Union army finally descended on the Navajo Nation, the Lord's only official representative had high-tailed out of sight.

Padre Damasio Taladrid, the campaign's chaplain, had been taking not only the soldiers' confessions but also their money, at least until he was ordered to stop playing monte with enlisted men. No one had complained about it when he served the armies of Spain and Mexico; still, Taladrid grudgingly accepted the U.S. military's rules about fraternization. What he could not tolerate were the questions about his drinking. Asked to sign a letter promising to abstain, the padre resigned his commission, riding off with his Bible and a pack of forty cards.[112]

So much the better for Major Arthur Morrison, one of the campaign's top commanders. After all, Father Taladrid had made a fuss about soldiers bringing prostitutes into camp, going so far as to file a formal complaint. Morrison, on the other hand, considered prostitution his calling. Once, after getting so drunk he could no longer stand, he boasted to his fellow soldiers, "I am the damnedest best pimp in New Mexico!"[113]

The officer who reported Morrison for that incident, Lieutenant David McCallister, was himself forced to resign a few months later, after he was found drunk in bed with an enlisted man. At the time he was serving as Fort Canby's officer of the day.[114]

Over at Fort Wingate, the officer in charge of the commissary, Lieutenant Archibald McEachran, resigned rather than face trial for drinking on duty. A few weeks later, the army discovered that addled or not, McEachran had managed to embezzle $1,400 in government funds. He was last seen headed for California, "drinking hard."[115]

The campaign against the Navajo lasted about nine months, and by its close in 1864, nearly half of the officers involved either had been brought up on charges or resigned to avoid them.

The only soldier to die in the climactic assault on Canyon de Chelly, Major Joseph Cummings, was an inveterate gambler who'd enlisted after the Confederates withdrew. When a search party found Cummings's body—he'd slipped out of camp without permission—they also discovered the $5,301 he was carrying at the time of his death.[116]

It was an inexplicable sum for an army officer in those days, but perhaps not so much for a slave trader. The demand for captives reached its apex during the U.S. onslaught of 1863–64, with young Navajo girls fetching $400 or more in the markets of Taos.[117]

Captain Albert Pfeiffer—the officer who led the final U.S. charge through Canyon de Chelly—knew all about kidnapping and enslaving Diné children. As the government's Ute subagent in Abiquiú, Pfeiffer had been sanctioning private slaving expeditions into Navajo country for several years, including the abduction of twenty-three Diné children that preceded the Navajo attack on Fort Defiance.[118]

According to the 1860 census, Pfeiffer and his wife personally held at least eight Natives in servitude at their home. Two Navajo children in his possession, a boy and a girl, were baptized in Taos as late as April 1862.[119]

The son of a Dutch minister, Pfeiffer first sailed to America at the age of twenty-two. Like countless other European immigrants, he set his sights on the western frontier, enlisting in the army and eventually winning an appointment as the government's Ute subagent in Abiquiú. He helped form the First New Mexico Volunteer Infantry Regiment when the war began, serving as a captain.

Along the way, Pfeiffer married a young woman of Spanish descent, with charcoal eyes and wealthy parents. They were soaking in a mineral spring when Apache fighters found them in the summer of 1863. Hit in the leg

Left: Captain Albert Pfeiffer sanctioned slave raids against Diné women and children and later led the U.S. assault on Canyon de Chelly. *Palace of the Governors.*

Right: Colonel Kit Carson weaponized slavery against the Navajo Nation in 1863, six months after Lincoln issued the Emancipation Proclamation. *Library of Congress.*

with an arrow, Captain Pfeiffer could only watch as the raiders made off with his wife. Her body was recovered a few miles away. Years later, he would acknowledge how the experience changed him, boasting that hungry wolves learned to trail him as he wandered through the mountains, searching for random Apache to kill.[120]

Yet just six months after Pfeiffer lost his wife, the army entrusted him to lead its first all-out assault on Canyon de Chelly. Instead of a uniform, Pfeiffer wore a massive buckskin coat, adorned with the beadwork of the Ute mercenaries he recruited to help attack the Navajo.

Pfeiffer's immediate supervisor—both at the Ute Agency and during the campaign against the Navajo—was the legendary Lieutenant Colonel Christopher "Kit" Carson. A short, bow-legged, fifty-four-year-old Missourian, Carson was celebrated in popular books of the era for helping to open the West. The cover of one, titled *The Fighting Trapper, or Kit Carson to the Rescue*, depicted him with a dagger in each hand, killing two warriors at the same time.

Carson, who could not read or write, did not need to embellish his life story. He'd spent decades working as a trapper, explorer and guide, learning the land when it was still under Mexican control and leading U.S. efforts to wrest it away in the 1840s.

Carson settled in northern New Mexico before it was even a U.S. territory, marrying Josefa Jaramillo, the fifteen-year-old daughter of a prominent Taos family (he was thirty-three at the time). After the war, Carson joined a business partner in claiming more than one million acres of Ute land to develop.[121] He also served as the federal government's liaison to the Ute, distributing shipments of tools, clothing and other goods.

In 1854, Carson was formally appointed Indian agent at Fort Garland, an outpost eighty miles north of Taos. The land there was so pristine that Americans hadn't even named it yet. In 1859, settlers were so desperate for governance that they announced the formation of "Jefferson Territory." Congress publicly ignored them but began drafting legislation to create the Territory of Colorado, which was formally established in early 1861.

Like Pfeiffer, Carson personally participated in the illegal slave trade. Church records show that he and Josefa held at least two young Navajo captives at their home in Taos in the 1860s.[122]

When the Civil War began in 1861, Carson helped organize the First New Mexico Volunteer Infantry Regiment, where Pfeiffer served as a captain. After the rebels withdrew, Carson was approached by Carleton to lead the campaigns against the Mescalero Apache and Navajo. Carson demurred at first and later tried to resign. But Carleton refused to let him go, determined to have his campaign led by the famous "Indian fighter."

At full strength, Carson's force numbered 736 men, organized into six mounted companies and three more of infantry. For the assault on Canyon de Chelly, intended to compel the Diné's unconditional surrender, he assigned 389 troopers of the First New Mexico Cavalry.

Carson received approval to augment his Union army columns with two hundred Ute mercenaries. He waited until after operations against the Navajo began to disclose to Carleton how he intended to pay the fighters: with captured Navajo women and children.

In weaponizing slavery, Carson hoped to speed the destruction of the Navajo Nation's collective identity. Six months after President Abraham Lincoln issued the Emancipation Proclamation, declaring enslaved people free in the Confederate South, Carson touted to Carleton the benefits of selling Navajo women and children into servitude:

Dear General,

I send by Captain Cutler the official report of the operations of my command since leaving Los Lunas, but in it have made no mention of the women and children captured by the Utes (4 women and 17 children). It is expected by the Utes, and has, I believe, been customary, to allow them to keep the women and children and the property captured by them for their own use and benefit, and as there is no other way to sufficiently recompense these Indians for their invaluable services, and as a means of insuring their continued zeal and activity, I ask it as a favor that they may be permitted to retain all that they may capture. I make this request the more readily as I am satisfied that the future of the captives disposed of in this manner would be much better than if sent even to the Bosque Redondo. As a general thing, the Utes dispose of their captives to Mexican families, where they are fed and taken care of, and thus cease to require any further attention on the part of the Government. Besides this, their being distributed as servants through the Territory causes them to lose that collectiveness of interest as a tribe which they will retain if kept together at any one place. Will you please let me know your views on this matter as soon as possible, that I may govern my conduct accordingly?

The Utes more than come up to the expectations I had formed of their efficiency as spies, nor can any small straggling parties of Navajos hope to escape them. I trust you will grant me permission to send Captain Pfeiffer to their villages to employ some more of them.[123]

Such was the tenor of the times and the temper of the men whom the United States placed in charge of prosecuting its war against the Navajo. Columns of wood, leather and horseflesh rumbled all through Navajo country that summer, fall and winter, striking at Steamboat Canyon, Ganado, Wide Ruins and beyond.

Diné families abandoned their hogans and went into hiding. The invaders laid waste to everything they found, burning corn fields, uprooting peach orchards and slaughtering thousands of sheep. In the end, it wasn't the Americans' guns that triumphed, but rather their willingness to target women, children and elderly alike. Diné families had nothing to eat and nowhere to hide, and winter was fast approaching. Slavery, starvation, exposure—it all served the same end:

Come dress your ranks, my gallant souls, a-standing in a row;
Kit Carson he is waiting to march against the foe!

Johnny Navajo—O Johnny Navajo!
We'll first chastise, then civilize, bold Johnny Navajo!

The army's ranks swelled with volunteers pulled from the surrounding colonial settlements—men like Chaves, who considered the Diné blood enemies. Some showed a propensity for violence that shocked their own comrades. An officer from New England, Captain Eben Everett, wrote in his personal journal:

> *August 22, 1863:…We started again for Canon De Chelle. Passed by the body of the Indian killed yesterday and found the scull bare, every particle of hair having been taken off making at least a dozen scalp locks. This style of proceeding may inaugurate retaliation and a system of warfare in which we may be sufferers. The Navajoes seldom or never scalp their prisoners and the barbarous practice should not have been commenced by us.*[124]

Native communities that didn't join in attacks on the Navajo were warned by the Americans to stand clear. In September 1863, Carleton wrote to Carson:

> *I recommend unless you can produce the same results by more gentle measures that you seize six of the principal men of the Zuni Indians and hold them hostage until all Navajoes in or near the village are given up, and all stolen stock surrendered. You will assure the Zuni Indians that if I hear they help or harbor Navajoes, or steal stock from any white man, I will as certainly destroy their village as sure as the sun shines.*[125]

By then, Carleton had already denied Carson's request to compensate Ute fighters with Navajo captives, insisting that all prisoners be sent to Bosque Redondo. "There must be no exceptions to this rule," he wrote. Carleton restated the policy in another letter to Carson in September 1863, this time emphasizing that the rule applied not just to Ute fighters but to American troops as well:

> *I have received the report of your operations in the vicinity of Cañon de Chelly. If any Indians desire to give themselves up, they will be received*

and sent to Fort Wingate, with a request they be sent to Los Pinos. No Navajoe Indians of either sex, or of any age, will be retained at Fort Canby as servants, or in any capacity whatsoever. All must go to the Bosque Redondo.[126]

Four months later, Carleton amplified the message to Carson, still worried soldiers were retaining captives as servants:

If you have more than a hundred captives <u>bring them all</u>. Do not leave in Fort Canby, as servants or otherwise, one single man, woman, or child, of any tribe. And when you come by Fort Wingate, make a clean sweep of every Indian man, woman, or child, whether held as servants or otherwise, at that post.[127]

The contradiction of allowing Diné families to be enslaved in New Mexico—while simultaneously fighting another war to free Black slaves in the South—was not lost on everyone. In October 1863, Lieutenant Colonel Samuel Tappan was given command of Fort Garland in southern Colorado, where Carson had established the Ute agency ten years earlier. Tappan was a lifelong abolitionist. Before the war, he'd participated in the Underground Railroad, helping enslaved people escape through Kansas to free northern states.

Upon his arrival at Fort Garland, Tappan was appalled to find that America had another, illegal slave system operating in plain sight. He discovered that Carson's replacement as Ute agent—a close friend of Albert Pfeiffer's named Lafayette Head—was encouraging slave raids. Tappan later recalled:

In the fall of 1863 while in command of Fort Garland, Colorado Territory, I received information which satisfied me of the complicity of Lafayette Head, Agent to the Ute Indians in the kidnapping and enslaving of Navajo Indian women and children, and who by his example encouraged the Mexican population to engage in this infamous business. The attention of the Government was called to the fact and an investigation ordered. Head succeeded in proving that the Navajo women and children in his family were purchased by his wife as an act of charity, etc.[128]

It didn't seem like an act of charity to Head's sister. She visited his compound around that same time and was so outraged by the treatment

Colonel Samuel Tappan was rebuffed by fellow officers when he reported that five hundred raiders "recently left for the purpose of taking Navajoe Captives." *Library of Congress.*

of his Diné captives that she helped one to escape. Head's nephew, Finis E. Downing, later recalled:

> *Mother hated the system, and the cries of the poor girl when beaten with rawhide whip until she was bleeding and bruised was more than Mother could stand. She planned a prison delivery and with her own hand turned the key and provided the horse that carried the Indian girl back to her people. The horse was mysteriously returned in a few days, with a note of thanks crudely written, tied to the mane of the horse. This opened the row good and plenty and mother determined to return to Illinois. All necessary arrangements for the trip were made by my Uncle Lafe. I was very much opposed to coming back. I liked the country and was much attached to my clear old Uncle Lafe, who had arranged for my education at a Santa Fe college. But I was for Mother against everything and her pleas always won with me. On the 12th of November, 1863, we started home in a sort of carriage bus to Denver.*[129]

Back at Fort Garland, Tappan continued to sound the alarm about New Mexico's slave trade. In January 1864, just as Carson and Pfeiffer were staging their final assault on Canyon de Chelly, Tappan asked his counterparts in New Mexico for help interdicting slavers, reporting that a company five hundred strong had just departed for Navajo country:

I have the honor to report to the General Commanding Dept. of New Mexico, that a Navajoe Boy captured by the Mexicans, has recently fallen into my hands. I wish to assertain [sic] *if it is the intention of General Carleton to colonize Navajoe captives; if so, it is my desire to send this Boy at first opportunity back to his tribe wherever it may be; in the mean time I shall consider him as a prisoner, and myself in the disposal of him, subject to the orders of the General commanding Dept. of New Mexico.*

I have also to report that a considerable traffic has been going on for years, among the Mexicans and Ute Indians, in the buying and selling of Navajoe Women and Children, and the necessity of an order to prevent a longer continuance of such disgraceful practices: the prices paid by the Mexicans for Navajoe Children is from $100 to $300 each, and a higher price for women, who are reduced to slavery. This system is in direct violation of law, and in opposition to the policy of our Government towards the different Indian Tribes, and as there is but little doubt, but what the "Federal Government" will, sooner or later put a stop to this traffic, declare its victims free, without remuneration to their imagined owners, involving a considerable loss to the Mexicans, and occasion serious difficulty with them, in consequence of their having been so long encouraged to invest their money in such purchases, until they imagine that they have a right in "fee simple" to all Navajoes they are able to buy. It is for the interests of the Mexicans that they should be warned in time, that they understand the risks they run in this business.

A letter from Hon. Wm. P. Dole, Indian Commissioner, just received, assures me of the determination of the Government to correct this flagrant abuse, and that steps have been taken already, to assertain the truth of the matter, with a view to its entire suppression.

I am informed that parties are making preparations at Abiquiu in New Mexico, for a private campaign against the Navajoes, claiming that they are authorized to do so by an old Mexican law, or the order of the Executive of New Mexico, and that nearly five-hundred (some of them from Conejas Co. in this Territory) recently left for the purpose of taking Navajoe Captives, for which they expect to find a ready market in which to sell them as slaves. Unless these men are in a measure controlled by military law, and orders from Dept. Hd. Qrs, sufficient to prevent them from selling their captives, but to hold them as prisoners of war, and subject to the control of the General Commanding the Dept. of New Mexico, I shall report the matter to the Government for its action.[130]

Images of Navajo slaves greeting visitors at Kit Carson's command post. One of his captives, renamed Juan Carson, is shown at left. *Fort Garland Museum.*

Tappan waited more than a month for a reply. The answer finally came from Major Cyrus de Forrest, General Carleton's aide-de-camp. De Forrest got straight to the point: army commanders in New Mexico would be happy to relieve Tappan of the Diné youth, but they had no interest in stopping the slave raids:

> *Respectfully esteemed to the writer who will please forward the captive boy he speaks of to Santa Fe where this boy will be sent to join his tribe at Fort Sumner. If the people of Colorado are going out after Navajo women and children to sell them, would it not be wise for Col. Tappan to write to his Dept. Com'er on this subject?*[131]

There would be no help for the Diné. The slave system that began under the conquistadors was about to reach its zenith—encouraged by agents of the U.S. government.

In the fall of the 1863, after soldiers destroyed the peach orchards of Canyon de Chelly, Delgadito and Barboncito made one last bid for peace. Their brother, Sordo, was among two emissaries who arrived at Fort Wingate on October 17 to present a new offer. To prove their peacefulness, they

The caption of this 1975 postcard claims that the Navajo "came to respect Kit Carson and the 1st New Mexico Cavalry." *Author's collection.*

8

PRIVATE, FIELD DRESS
FIRST NEW MEXICO VOLUNTEER
CAVALRY REGIMENT
1864

This volunteer regiment was raised in northern New Mexico, at the outset of the Civil War. Composed of both Anglo's and native Spanish-Americans, these soldiers served at Fort Union in 1861, and in 1864 to 1866. Colorful Kit Carson, the famed frontiersman, was the regimental colonel for four years—as well as commanding officer of Fort Union for five months. The troopers campaigned for long, hard months, and compiled a sustained and successful combat record against many hostile tribes in this area. The Navahos, Mescalero Apaches, Comanches, and Kiowas all came to respect Kit Carson and the 1st New Mexico Cavalry.

© K/S HISTORICAL PUBLICATIONS, Saddle River, N.J. 1975

PLACE
STAMP
HERE

ITI
Spring Valley,
N.Y.

offered to move their entire band close to the fort, next to a spring known as the Gallina.

Fort Wingate's commander, Captain Rafael Chacón, sent a report to Carleton the next day, offering to kill them all if they refused to go to Bosque Redondo:

Fort Wingate N.M., Oct. 18, 1863.

General:

I have the honor to report to you that yesterday two Navajoe Indians one of them called Sordo and the other Pedro Sarracino came to this fort. The first is the brother of Barboncito & Delgadito and the other belongs to their villages. These Indians desire to make peace and request the General Comd'g to allow them to establish themselves in a place which may be assigned them.

They offer themselves to arrest all delinquents of their tribe, or to fight against them in company with the troops, until they are subdued or destroyed. The number of the Indians who desire this, is I believe, five hundred; men, women, and children. They furthermore have said that while the answer of the General is coming, they will under all circumstances establish themselves in the Gallina, and if they should not be looked upon as peaceful Indians, that they should go as far as Santa Fé to sue for peace, even if the whole of them should be assassinated.

I understand that these Indians will come here within nine days, and if the General Comd'g should order them to go to Santa Fé or any other place they will go; and if they should not do so, our troops are ready to execute them.[132]

Carleton sent a response three days later, via Assistant Adjutant General Ben Cutler:

In reply I am directed by the Department Commander to say that the Navajoe Indians have no choice in this matter; they must come in and go to the Bosque Redondo, or remain in their own country and be at war.[133]

Sordo and Barboncito were steadfast: they would stay in their own country, whatever the cost. Delgadito thought otherwise. He considered the scorched fields, coming snows and desperate faces and decided that the cost was too high already.

Delgadito could not be sure what awaited them if they surrendered, but he knew what was coming if they didn't. In November 1863, he rode to Fort Wingate with 187 members of his band and agreed to go to Bosque Redondo.

HWÉELDI'

L ike many of the soldier-miners of the California Column, Lieutenant
William Wardwell never gave up the dream of striking it rich in New
Mexico.

After helping to drive Confederates from the territory, Wardwell and
six of his comrades filed claim on a silver deposit along the western slopes
of the Magdalena Mountains.[134] Yet it wasn't minerals that eventually
made Wardwell a wealthy man—it was sugar, tobacco, whiskey and meat
pies. He set himself up as the sutler at Fort Craig after the war, supplying
soldiers with extra rations, tools and anything else they wanted. By the
time the 1870 census takers came around, Wardwell was the wealthiest
California veteran in the territory, with a reported net worth of $65,000.[135]
Not bad for a man who got his start serving coffee and bread to 188 Navajo
prisoners, most of whom had never tasted coffee or bread before.

About two weeks after Delgadito's surrender in November 1863, his
party arrived in Santa Fe in the custody of Captain Rafael Chacón and
his New Mexico volunteers. Carleton—perhaps recalling Chacón's offer
the previous month to massacre Delgadito's entire band—arranged for
Wardwell and a detail of California volunteers to escort them the rest of
the way to Bosque Redondo.

Having spent months calling for the Diné's destruction, the general's focus
turned to Delgadito's comfort. He asked his officers to procure tender beef for
the prisoners and a few of the stove-warmed tents patented by the Confederate
turncoat who once attacked Delgadito's band, Henry Sibley:

See that they have rations of flour, meat, salt, and half rations of sugar and coffee. See that they are treated with great kindness. Let Captain Fritz have four worn Sibley tents for the use of the women and children. These will be transferred to the acting assistant quartermaster at Fort Sumner.

The meat ration had better be beeves on the hoof as far as practicable. In this event gentle cattle should be selected. You will please give your personal attention to see that these Indians are well cared for, and if you have not got the worn tents, this is your authority for drawing them from the depot quartermaster.[136]

That same afternoon, Carleton wrote a second set of instructions for Major Henry Wallen, the commanding officer at Fort Sumner and Bosque Redondo:

Today one hundred and eighty eight men, women, and children of the Navajoe tribe of Indians, leave Santa Fe for the Bosque Redondo, via Fort Union. I beg you will take particular pains to have these Indians located in a good place—and to see they have some shelter for their women and children. I learn that others have come in to Fort Wingate. These will soon be forwarded to you. Among the Indians who leave here today is Delgadito.

I have promised that he, and three others, named Cha-hay, Chiquito, and Tsee-é, shall return at once with the interpreter Jesus to the Navajo country, to let other Navajoes know what kind of a place the tribe is expected to move to, and to let the tribe know how those are treated who have gone to that point. Let those four Indians and Jesus have passports to return at once to Fort Wingate. The government seems to take great interest in this experiment of placing the nomadic Indians on reservations, and this exodus of the Navajo people from their country, to become a domesticated race, is an interesting subject to us all, and one fraught with great questions so far as the prospective wealth and advancement of New Mexico may go. Of course, the subject of timely preparation of acequias and of grounds for next year's crops will demand and receive your earnest attention.[137]

Delgadito left Santa Fe around noon on November 22. He was still riding his own horse, albeit under the watchful eye of Lieutenant Wardwell. With most of the other prisoners riding in wagons, the group made good time, covering eight miles before they stopped for the evening. As the Diné ate their supper, they could see clouds gathering in the distance—male clouds, dark and volatile, telling them that a storm was coming.

By sunrise, eight inches of snow had fallen, slowing the caravan's progress to seven miles a day, moving from sunup to sundown. On the fifth day, they awoke near Tecolote to find some of the cattle gone. They waited for the soldiers to round up the strays, finally getting underway again around noon. They'd been moving east until this point; now Wardwell turned them north, toward Fort Union, which they finally reached on November 30, eight days after leaving Santa Fe.[138]

They took on fresh supplies there, including several of the tent and stove sets developed by Henry Sibley; Carleton's insistence on them appears to be the only reason they headed north to Fort Union before backtracking south, toward Fort Sumner and Bosque Redondo.

Of all the routes taken to Bosque Redondo, that first one was the longest and most arduous, spanning 498 miles of steep and winding trail, just as winter set in. Yet the greatest danger wasn't weather—it was slave traders. Soldiers were strung out along the trail, leaving some of the wagons unprotected. By the time they reached Fort Sumner, fifteen members of Delgadito's party were missing, most of them apparently stolen by slavers.[139]

Soldiers never learned to protect their convoys of prisoners. In months to come, scores more would be lost to slavers during a series of forced marches to Bosque Redondo, which collectively became known as the Long Walk of the Navajo.

Upon arriving at Fort Sumner, Delgadito discovered that it was less fort than campsite. Only a few buildings had been finished. Hwéeldi', the Diné called it, possibly derived from the Spanish word for fort, *fuerte*. The soldiers, most of them volunteers from California and New Mexico, slept in small tents, ate in the open and complained pitifully in letters back home. One wrote:

> *It is on the verge of civilization. Anton Chico, the nearest settlement, is 90 miles distant. All news reaches us a month after it has been made known to all mankind. The insufferable dullness and stupidity of the place is occasionally relieved by the vigorous Indian scout and by keeping a bright watch on the Texan frontier in order to promptly and effectively repulse an invasion from that Quarter.*[140]

The troops' primary role was to act as a deterrence: to keep the rebels in Texas and to keep the Diné from leaving the vast, barren and wall-less prison. When Delgadito arrived, he found that the camp already housed about four hundred Mescalero Apache, or Ndé. The Ndé and Diné are historically

Vast but barren, Bosque Redondo could not support the nine thousand Diné men, women and children interred there from 1863 to 1868. *Palace of the Governors.*

related—their languages are different branches of the Athabaskan tree—but relations were not always friendly in those days. Understandably, the Mescalero Apache at Bosque Redondo eyed the newcomers with suspicion.

Delgadito and his group were probably more disturbed to find another band of Diné there—or rather, the band of Diné Ana'aai, "Enemy Navajo." Based near Cebolleta, the group long ago turned their backs on the Navajo Nation and allied themselves with the colonizers. They collaborated with the Mexicans first and then the Americans. Some Diné Ana'aai served as scouts for the invaders and even participated in slave raids. Yet the treachery of the Diné Ana'aai earned them nothing; they were the first band of Navajo the U.S. Army forced out of Navajo country.

Bosque Redondo was a big place, so the army's plan was simply to ask the rival groups to avoid each other. Major Wallen provided Delgadito's group with warm tents, clean blankets and plenty of food, just as Carleton instructed.

Through interpreters, the soldiers explained that they wanted Delgadito to see for himself how safe and comfortable it was at Bosque Redondo. And now that he had seen it was so, they wanted him to leave—to go back to his own country and convince others to surrender. First, however, he should return to Santa Fe to meet with Carleton once again.

One of the Americans handed Delgadito something—paper with writing on it, much smaller than a treaty. A passport, they called it. If any soldiers stopped Delgadito on the way to Santa Fe, he could just show them the paper, and they would let him continue on his way.

Delgadito looked at the passport. *These Bilagáana and their papers.* In time, he'd come to know the document well, studying the contours of every word and symbol, learning how to replicate them. For now, though, he had a bigger problem. Somewhere out there, Carson's forces were still snaking through Dinétah. Delgadito's wife and children might be safe, but Sordo, Barboncito and thousands of others remained on the run, hunted by every soldier, slaver and vigilante in the territory. So, just days after arriving at Bosque Redondo, Delgadito agreed to go back out again.

PART III

BEAUTY AGAIN

HATH NOT WHERE TO LAY HIS HEAD

Delgadito arrived back in Santa Fe a few days before Christmas. Carleton, it turned out, was hoping for a gift.

As Delgadito sat inside the Palace of the Governors, listening to the general speak Bilagáana, waiting for one interpreter to translate the words into Spanish and another to translate them into Diné Bizaad, he realized something: *Carleton needed him.*

Now that Delgadito had surrendered, Carleton wanted him to go back to his own country, to spread word that it was safe it was to come to Bosque Redondo. More than that, he wanted Delgadito to personally lead the Diné there.

And yet, now that Delgadito had surrendered, Carleton had no leverage, no way to compel him to do anything. That's why this great general—with his gold epaulets, massive sideburns and imperious attitude—was suddenly doing something new: he was asking, not demanding. The warm tents, the tender beef—it all made sense now.

Delgadito seized the moment. He would agree but on one condition: Carleton must free the slaves. It was a remarkable request. Since 1846, Diné leaders had negotiated seven separate treaties with the United States, and not once had the return of their people been on the table.

Even more remarkable, the general agreed to his terms.[141] If Delgadito could persuade others to surrender, Carleton would force the settlers to give up their slaves. The Navajo would be together again, albeit as prisoners of Bosque Redondo.

It was a start. Military passport in hand, Delgadito set out with three other Diné riders on December 23, 1863. Carleton instructed his field commanders:

> *You will let Delgadito and the three Indians who are with him go out among their people, free to go where they please. But when they come back, if they should come back, they are not to be permitted to lurk around the post, but will be sent in with all the Indians who come in with them. I count on good results in letting these Indians run at large, for they will tell the others how we are treating those who have already surrendered. Let me know the day they leave your post to go out among their people.*[142]

Over the next few weeks, the four men navigated an icy war zone. Enemies were everywhere. Rumors were rampant that the bluecoats planned to massacre all the Diné at Bosque Redondo. Delgadito and his companions tried to assuage those fears. They warned that the most dangerous thing to do was to stay.

That same month, Carson and Pfeiffer embarked on their final assault on Canyon de Chelly. Delgadito's brother Sordo rushed to stop them. On January 12, 1864—the same day Carson arrived at the western mouth of Canyon de Chelly—Sordo was shot and scalped by the men of Company F, First New Mexico Volunteers.[143]

Around that same time, Delgadito arrived back at Fort Wingate with a caravan of Diné families ready to surrender. Hoping for more, Carleton expanded the scope of Delgadito's mission to include all Diné, everywhere. On January 15, Carleton's aide-de-camp, Cyrus DeForrest, instructed officers at Fort Wingate:

> *The general commanding directs me to say to you that Delgadito, having done so well in his recent trip into the Navajo country, need not be sent to the Bosque Redondo with the other Indians until further orders, but will be allowed to make other trips for the purpose of inducing more Navajoes to come in.*[144]

The following month, the *Santa Fe Gazette* incorrectly reported that Delgadito had been killed. The item appeared directly above a report praising Carson's attack on Canyon de Chelly:

> *DELGADITO: We regret to learn that the Navajo chief, Delgadito, has been killed. He was one of the most influential men in the tribe, and his influence*

was exerted at all times in favor of peace and good-neighborship with the whites. Indeed, the last information we had of him, before the arrival of the bad news of his death, was that he was exerting himself in bringing in his people to the Posts in the Navajo country and surrendering them to the authorities to be by them taken to Fort Sumner to be colonized; and he was succeeding well in his exertions. It is rarely that the word good can be used in connection with the word Navajo, but we presume it could with propriety have been used as a qualifying term to Delgadito.

He was killed in an attack made upon a rancheria in which he was, by an independent party of militia. It is said the fight was forced upon the rancheria and that the defense was well maintained by the Indians.

COL CARSON: On Wednesday of this week Col. Carson arrived in Santa Fe, from the Navajo Country, after an absence of several months during which time he has been strictly engaged in the prosecution of the Navajo war. The recent exploits which he with his command have performed, and which we have alluded to frequently, have added to his fame as an Indian fighter and will give him an enviable reputation as a commander of troops in the field.

He has beyond doubt broken the spirit of the Navajo nation to such an extent that the war will soon be brought to close, by the surrender of the tribe to the military authorities who will, in accordance with the policy inaugurated by Gen'l. Carleton, locate them at Fort Sumner on the Pecos river where many have already gone. This is "a consummation most devoutly to be wished," and when it shall have been accomplished the people of New Mexico will hail those who shall accomplish it as public benefactors. A few years of the peace which will succeed the subjugation of this tribe will place the people again on their feet and bring prosperity to the Territory.[145]

Upon seeing the false report of Delgadito's death, army commanders raced to set the record straight. One week after being told that Delgadito was dead, readers of the *Gazette* opened the paper to discover that Delgadito had survived an attack by Hispano raiders. The slavers tore up the party's passport, killed one of Delgadito's companions and fled with several Diné captives:

HEADQUARTERS, FORT WINGATE, N.M.
February 15th, 1864

MR. EDITOR: *The statement in your paper of February 13th that the Navajo Chief Delgadito was killed by the independent Militia is a mistake. Delgadito was coming in to this Post with some seven hundred of his people, men, women, and children, who as a matter of course were scattered over several miles of road. Their rear was attacked by a party of Mexicans, and I believe two or three killed and some prisoners taken. One of the Indians that came with Delgadito from Fort Sumner was killed. Delgadito himself is now on his way to Fort Sumner with a party of 750 Indians, and another party of 453 started before him—Delgadito requesting to remain until the last, and larger party was sent. I have sent 1203 Navajo Indians from this Post, in two parties, which have come in mainly through the influence of Delgadito. Delgadito's party was coming in, in good faith, and their safe guard from the Post was torn by the Mexican that it was shown too, and the Indian killed.*

I am Respectfully your Ob't. Servant
E.W. EATON,
Maj. 1st Cav. N.M. Vols.[146]

Included with Major Eaton's correction was a note from an anonymous "volunteer," written in a style that sounded an awful lot like Carleton's:

SIR: *Seeing it announced in your issue of the 13th that Delgadito had been killed, I deem it proper to inform you, that you have been misinformed. Since Delgadito's return from the Bosque Redondo, he has made two journeys from the Post into the Navajo Country, doing good service each time. On the last day of January there left this Post en route to the Bosque Redondo 1142 Indians (in addition to those brought from Canby by Col. Carson). On the same day Delgadito came in bringing with him nearly 800 Indians, from which time they have continued to arrive. On the 12th of present month 430 started from here under charge of Lt. Thos. Holmes, 1st Cav. N. M. Vols. On the 13th Delgadito and 750 more under charge of Lt. Campbell, 1st Cav. N. M. Vols, for Bosque Redondo. We have here now about 60, awaiting transportation. You see the good work goes bravely on. This Post alone has sent out 1340 Indians in less than 15 days time, and the cry is still they come. Delgadito is not dead, but is on his way rejoicing to the Bosque Redondo. Long may he live for he is a brave and a good man.*

He wishes to return once more to his old haunts for the purpose of saving as many of his people as possible from death at the hands of the Volunteers or from starvation, for of a certainty he says the red man hath not where to lay his head nor to stay his feet. Their strong holds have been invaded, their crops all destroyed and they themselves, have been obliged to eat horse flesh until but few horses are left them, therefore submit they must or starve.

Respectfully your Ob't. Servant,
VOLUNTEER[147]

Assuming that Carleton wrote the anonymous letter—and it's hard to imagine he didn't, given the mix of bombast and operational details—he was not entirely candid about the nature of Delgadito's final mission. On the same day the letter was published, Delgadito departed Fort Wingate not for Navajo country, but for some of the Spanish-speaking settlements. He'd held up his end of the bargain, and now Carleton was meeting his, allowing Delgadito one last mission before imprisonment at Bosque Redondo. One last ride back to where it all began, back to the slaves of Cebolleta, this time escorted by a small contingent of Union troops.

Led by a junior officer named Lieutenant George Campbell, they rode to Cubero first. Upon learning of their intentions, a priest there warned them to expect a fight. The padre, who had likely baptized some of the Navajo captives, couldn't imagine the settlers just giving up their slaves.

But the settlers did not resist, not at Cubero or Moquino, not even at Cebolleta. In all, ninety-five Diné captives were recovered from the settlements that week—the largest documented release of its kind. Even so, Campbell was convinced that the settlers were holding back. He wrote to Carleton:

[S]*ome of them submitted* [sic, here and throughout] *with a very bad grace to what they could not help and reluctantly gave up their peons I am confident in the belief that more peons are still in the vicinity of Sabietta* [Cebolleta] *but it is impossible to find them at present Maney of the inhabitants of this town will not give up their peons as long as they can keep them from the government and they will be closely watched until the last one of the india*[ns] *amongst them is discovered and removed, Much praise is due Lieut Stephens for the manner in which he conducted this somewhat delicate business, I certainly did not anticapat the finding of half the number that we brought away and as maney of these speak the Spanish language they will be very useful to the Government in the future.*[148]

Campbell was right; the 95 captives represented a fraction of the estimated 2,457 Diné who were baptized and held as servants during the decade.[149] Even those removed from settlements were not truly free. Like Delgadito, they were now prisoners of the U.S. government. But at least they were together.

To reach Bosque Redondo, Campbell led them south along the icy banks of the Rio San Jose, following it downstream to its juncture with the Rio Puerco. There they turned east, continuing across a stretch of desert strewn with basalt, the frozen fire of past volcanic eruptions.

Eventually, they reached the Rio Grande and the crossing at Los Pinos. For the first time, Delgadito could see the terrible scale of Carleton's operation. In a matter of weeks, the sleepy village had been transformed into a hub of forced migration, with exiles streaming in from every part of Dinétah. Many were barefoot, starving and suffering from exposure.

The slave raiders were there, too, waiting for a chance to strike, hoping to find a child who wandered off the trail or even a wagonload of unguarded prisoners. Sometimes the soldiers were complicit in kidnappings. In his report to Carleton, Lieutenant Campbell accused two of his fellow Union volunteers of selling off a young prisoner:

At this place officers who have indians in charge will have to exercise extreme vigilence or the indians children will be stolen from him and sold, And thier horses to[o] One boy was stolen from Lieut Lattimers comand and five horses from mine while awaiting transportation at Los Pinos, I have learned since on that road who sold this indian boy and as soon as I get to Wingate will place the facts before you, and the names of the tow [two] soldiers who has sold this boy.

I have been unable to learn the name of the man who bought him but from his discription I think I know him, I believe that direct proof can be had of this act which must exert a most pernicious influence on the indians under present circumstances.

Lieutenant Campbell reported one other crime at Los Pinos: the theft of Delgadito's belt. While Campbell does not describe the belt, he estimated its value at $100, a considerable sum in those days, such as one might expect for a finely crafted silver concho belt:

> *The theft was traced to some American soldiers, and there ended, I believe it to be no more than justice to yourself and all who have taken a part in this campaign that these thieves should be caught and punished if possable and shall take the earliest possable oportunity of bringing the whole matter before you.*[150]

There's no record of soldiers having been disciplined for the crimes Campbell reported. That same week, Carleton was busily preparing for the arrival of more prisoners at Bosque Redondo. He requested the army send 200,000 rations to Fort Sumner, estimating the size of the Navajo Nation at five thousand people, "all told."[151] If the general had guessed twice as many, he still would have come up short of the actual number, estimated at about fourteen thousand people.

Delgadito's efforts to reassure the Diné that Bosque Redondo was safe—safer than facing Carson's volunteers and mercenaries, anyway—had succeeded beyond all expectations. "Indeed," the historian Lawrence Kelly concluded after an analysis of campaign records, "Delgadito's peaceful mission was even more successful than Carson's in persuading the Navajo to surrender."[152]

Some Diné never surrendered, fleeing as far as the Grand Canyon to escape Carson's onslaught. Oral histories tell of hundreds of others climbing atop Fortress Rock, a nearly eight-hundred-foot-tall tower within Canyon del Muerto. Most, however, were now headed to Bosque Redondo—far more than the prison could sustain.

HUNGER

aptain Francis McCabe weighed the miles, the rations and the weather, and he knew they wouldn't make it. Not all of his eight hundred prisoners would reach Bosque Redondo alive.

They'd left Fort Canby on March 20, 1864, bound for Fort Wingate, Los Pinos and finally Fort Sumner. Two days out, a late snowstorm hit. McCabe reckoned that their rations—a pound of meat or flour per person, plus a half pound of bacon—was barely enough for the trip to Wingate. Rather than wait for the weather to subside, he ordered the prisoners to keep marching, although he'd later acknowledge that many "were nearly naked, and of course unable to withstand such a storm."[153]

The convoy included twenty-three supply wagons. McCabe ordered the oldest and sickest prisoners placed in twenty-two wagons; he left the last one empty, so it could trail the prisoners to pick up those who collapsed along the way.

On March 29, they reached Fort Wingate and obtained a fresh rations— but only half as much as before. McCabe later recalled:

Apprehensive that this unexpected diminution of their rations would have the effect of shaking their faith in the government, and of creating mistrust and suspicion which if not promptly removed might lead to serious consequences, I called the principal Chiefs and warrior together, and told them that I believed they would receive their full amount of rations at Los Pinos; and that the present diminution was but a temporary arrangement

*occasioned by the scarcity of provisions This seemed to satisfy them, and
they assured me that they would travel forward to the reservation.*

When they reached Los Pinos on April 4, McCabe procured four hundred
blankets for his prisoners, as well as some brass kettles for cooking. For some,
the supplies came too late. By the time the group reached Fort Sumner on
May 11, 110 of McCabe's prisoners had died of hunger or exposure. He
learned that a caravan that left Fort Canby two weeks earlier had fared even
worse—out of 2,500 prisoners, 197 died.[154] Those who survived relied on
ingenuity. They took their rations of flour, sugar and lard; put the kettles
over fire; and invented frybread, now considered a regional delicacy.

Back in Santa Fe, Carleton's moment of triumph was already falling apart.
The Diné were surrendering in numbers far beyond what he'd expected.
Carson and other field commanders now reported that the nation might
include as many as twelve thousand people, more than twice what Carleton
had expected. Notes of worry began to creep into the general's letters. A few
days before McCabe left Fort Canby, Carleton told Carson to instruct his
officers, "I think we can feed 6000 Navajoes, but not to send in more."[155] By
then it was too late; thousands more were already on the way.

Numbers became an obsession. Ration cards were distributed to control
the food supply. George Gwyther, the camp's surgeon, later recalled:

> *The number of the Navajoes on the reserve was an uncertain one, rendered so
> by births, deaths, arrivals, and the temporary absence of some. Usually the
> number present approximated nine thousand; but to obtain a precise estimate
> for each month, the plan of collecting them together as they passed through a
> gate into a large corral was established; and to prevent their strong tendency
> to duplication, it was found necessary to keep them all in there until all were
> counted, issuing to each single person, or head of family, a ticket indicating the
> number of rations to which his circumstances entitled him.*[156]

His circumstances…or Carleton's. As the general's concern over supplies
edged toward panic, he began cutting the size of rations, and he kept
cutting. One of the camp's top commanders, Major Henry Wallen, finally
refused to cut anymore. On April 1, 1864, Wallen sat down to write a
report explaining why he'd defied Carleton's orders:

> *On the 26th of last month I issued half rations to the Indians.…For the past
> 2 or 3 days they have been begging for food, and loud in their complaints.*

Yesterday I again issued to them, and the ravenous manner with which they seized their portion, added to what I had already seen and their previous complaints, caused me to make a thorough inspection of their condition, in which I was assisted by the Surgeon of the Post. The suffering even to actual starvation was terrible, and I have assumed the responsibility of an issue of full rations to them....I am now compelled to issue [rations] every third day. The school children receive their portion each day at school, which ensures a large attendance. In addition to the necessity of full rations for these people on the score of humanity, I have to urge upon your attention my belief that, if half rations were persisted in for a week longer, nearly all the men, certainly those without families, would leave the reservation, and with my present force, I cannot detain them. They are now taunting Delgadito and their other chiefs with having brought them here to starve, say that they have been lied to, and that they can steal enough to keep them from starving. Some of them are openly (among themselves) counseling the others to leave....I must strenuously urge upon you the necessity of giving them plenty of food, and of sending me a sufficient force particularly of cavalry to detain them on the reservation, and to guard against any possible treachery.[157]

The shortage of rations wasn't Carleton's only problem. James Collins, the supportive publisher of the *Santa Fe Gazette*, had been replaced as the territory's superintendent of Indian affairs. The new superintendent, a Pennsylvania physician named Michael Steck, not only questioned the need to exile the Navajo, but he also made clear that his agency wouldn't be paying for it. If Carleton wanted a reservation, the War Department could pay for it. Steck and the Department of the Interior wanted no part of it.

Meanwhile, Colonel Tappan, the abolitionist commander of Fort Garland in Colorado Territory, was continuing to make noise about the slave trade in New Mexico. Unable to get Carleton to act, he'd written directly to U.S. Commissioner of Indian Affairs William P. Dole. Dole forwarded Tappan's letter to Steck, wanting to know if the allegations of widespread slavery were true. Steck backed every word of it:

In reply I would state that the letter referred to exposes clearly and truthfully the condition of about two thousand Indians in New Mexico, belonging principally to the Navajo Tribe, but including also Apaches, Pah Utahs, and Pueblos.

I agree with him also as to the bad influence the traffic in Navajo children has had upon that tribe, and that no permanent peace can be had

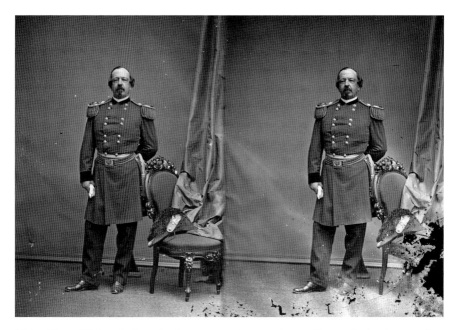

Major Henry Wallen disobeyed orders to cut prisoner rations at Bosque Redondo, reporting that the "suffering even to actual starvation was terrible." *Library of Congress.*

with them as long as this evil is permitted. The Navajos are a powerful tribe, and are noted for their ingenuity and industry. They cultivate wheat and corn extensively, manufacture excellent blankets, and own large herds of sheep. And if properly treated it can certainly be made in their interest to cease marauding, and remain at peace in their own country, they having much to lose in the event of a protracted war. They will not, however, be controlled while their children are stolen, bought, and sold by our people.

Of the probable number, two thousand, now in the hands of the people of New Mexico, many have been captured recently, while others have served from childhood to old age; it is therefore an evil that has existed for many years.

The price that has usually been paid for captives is about $100, but frequently after becoming domesticated, they sell much higher. They are usually adopted into the family, baptized, and brought up in the Catholic faith and given the name of the owner's family, generally become faithful and trustworthy servants, and sometimes are married to the native New Mexican.

There is no law of the Territory that legalizes the sale of Indians, yet it is done almost daily, without an effort stop it.[158]

The "law of the territory"—that was another headache for Carleton. The continuance of martial law initially had been accepted by most residents as the cost of war, but as time passed and the threat of a second Confederate invasion faded, complaints grew. Carleton's requirement that residents carry military-issued passports became a particular sore point. "The Civic Nose Is Again Brought to the Military Grindstone," declared a headline in the *Santa Fe Weekly New Mexican*, which derided Carleton as "Major Pomposo."

One of Carleton's fiercest critics was Joseph Knapp, a justice of the territorial Supreme Court. In August 1863, Knapp was arrested and thrown in an army guardhouse for five days because he refused to carry Carleton's passport, which he considered a violation of civilian rule. Knapp escalated his protest during the court's next term by simply staying home, paralyzing the January 1864 proceedings.

When the court reconvened the following July, Knapp was back on the bench, but not to hear cases. His fellow justice, Kirby Benedict, wrote to President Lincoln to complain:

> *Each day he delivered speeches from his seat on the bench to all present against Carleton and the military in New Mexico. His mind seemed in a Quixotic whenever the military are in his thoughts. His speeches were made with such warmth and he used very strong expressions.*[159]

Lincoln removed Knapp from the court that month but could do nothing to silence the judge, who continued to attack Carleton in the press and his personal correspondence. Months after leaving the bench, Knapp accused Carleton's troops of wholesale slaughter, writing to Commissioner Dole:

> *I live here in the country of the Apache, and can speak from facts within my knowledge, when I say that the "plan" has proved the worst thing which could have taken place. Towards the Apache the "plan" is executed by killing every one which can be seen—a war of extermination, reaching to the women and children.*[160]

Most New Mexicans remained untroubled by Carleton's tactics; they celebrated the exodus of the Navajo and Mescalero Apache from their midst. To commemorate the event, Governor Henry Connelly proclaimed the first Thursday in April 1864 as a day of prayer and thanksgiving. Bells chimed from Santa Fe's church steeples.

Carleton, however, could not escape the grim math of Bosque Redondo. Once again, he moved to reduce rations. Going over Wallen's head this time, he instructed General Marcellus Crocker in October 1864 to cut rations twice in the same week. He wrote Crocker:

> *But a few days since I wrote to you directing that the ration of breadstuffs to be issued until further orders, to each captive Indian, big and little, upon the reservation, must be cut down to one pound and a quarter per day.*
>
> *Since that was written I have had consultations with the chief commissary with reference to his ability to get an adequate supply of stores to the Bosque, so that there would be no danger of running short, and I find that in my judgment it is all-important to reduce the ration of breadstuff to 12 ounces per day, and to have issued 8 ounces of meat per day—20 ounces of solid food in all.... We shall strain every nerve to get a plenty; but as we may encounter delays which would perhaps be fatal to the Indians, unless this precaution were taken, the Indians must see the necessity which compels it and be satisfied. Assemble the chiefs and tell them this:*
>
> *1ˢᵗ. That we did not look for a loss of all their corn by the worms, but supposed that they would raise nearly enough this year to support themselves, which they have failed to do.*
>
> *2ⁿᵈ. That we have been greatly embarrassed in getting their supplies from the States because the Kiowas and Comanches attacked our train.*
>
> *3ʳᵈ. That the hail and frost killed nearly all the corn in Taos and Mora, the 2 places where we expected to get what the Indians would need.*
>
> *4ᵗʰ. That more Indians have come in than we expected would come, which must be fed.*
>
> *5ᵗʰ. That they must make their food into atole, by which it will go much further, and use the pumpkins and melons, of which Mr. Labadie informs me there are yet many, to help out their meals. The Indians must be made to understand that we are doing our best for them, but cannot overcome impossibilities; that unless we took this timely precaution they must starve.*[161]

As 1864 came to a close, Captain McCabe set about preparing the first U.S. census report on the Navajo Nation. He reported a total of 8,354

Diné prisoners at Bosque Redondo, a third of them children. Forecasting a bright future, he made no mention of the crop failures, food shortages and dysentery now plaguing the camp:

> *Transported as these Indians are from their native land a distance of over 400 miles, they will necessarily cherish old recollections for a few years; but under a firm and just government they will soon become reconciled, and even attached, to their present location.*[162]

McCabe, a cavalry officer, took particular interest in three thousand horses brought to Bosque Redondo. The Navajo, branded as rustlers, turned out to be excellent breeders:

> *The horses belonging to the tribe are of a small but well-formed breed, very hardy, and sometimes possessing great speed and power of endurance. In their forays upon the settlements the marauders were enabled to defy their pursuers owing to the good quality of their horses. They will average twelve hands in height, and require little or no grain, but obtain their support from the nutritious game grass that abounds in the neighborhood of the reservation. As there is a great proportion of mares among them, a few years will develop a large increase of this species of stock; and it is not going too far to predict that at no distant day our cavalry in this department may be entirely remounted on horses of the Navajo breed.*

By McCabe's count, the prisoners also had 6,962 sheep and 630 looms:

> *They fabricate a strong and durable cloth and elegant blankets of a variety of patterns and brilliant colors, for which purposes the Navajoes value the wool they obtain from their sheep. These fabrics are made in hand looms of simple construction by the women of the tribe. One industrious female can finish a blanket in three weeks, which will wear for ten years, is perfectly waterproof, and will command a price as high as $50 to $200.*

The blankets' value went far beyond that. To the knowing eye, every Navajo weaving tells a story. Hundreds of miles from home, the looms became tools of cultural preservation and the weavers, guardians of tradition. It's said that their ancestors first learned the art from Spider Woman; some wonder how they would have survived the years in exile without it. Lynda Teller Pete—a Diné author, teacher and fifth-generation weaver—has observed:

An 1865 report noted 630 looms at Bosque Redondo, offering a means of cultural preservation as well as protection from the elements. *Library of Congress.*

Weaving represents our connection to the universe, holding our stories, our prayers, and our songs—told, chanted, sung, and preserved in the weaving motions. Each weaver is unique. I touch tapestries woven by my grandmothers, mother, sisters, niece, nephew, and granddaughter. I see their hands strumming the warps, I hear the resonating beats of their weaving combs, and without seeing them, I know who is weaving just by their beats.[163]

McCabe took note of another talent on display at Bosque Redondo, one he found particularly promising:

There are several men in the tribe who are skilled to a certain extent in blacksmithing, making bridle bits and other articles of horse equipage in a creditable manner. As soon as one or two forges are established on the reservation the ingenuity of these self-taught sons of Vulcan will have ample room for development.

Ample room indeed. As soon as one or two forges were established, the Diné smiths would have everything needed to begin forging military passports and ration tickets.

McCabe could not have foreseen what was coming, yet in the same report, he singled out their future ringleader for special attention. Identifying Delgadito as one of the "principal chiefs," McCabe wrote, "This man is reliable, intelligent, and can write his signature legibly."

THE BLACKSMITH'S SHOP

The chief quartermaster will direct that a set of blacksmith tools complete, and some iron, be sent to Fort Sumner for the use of the Navajoes. Tell them to go to work at once and make adobes to build the shop. You select the site near the post, and have the shop made long enough to have a forge in each end.
—Captain Ben Cutler, Fort Sumner, New Mexico, August 1864[164]

It's not clear when the forgeries began, but in early 1865, soldiers working in Fort Sumner's commissary discovered that their ration tickets had been altered, allowing for more food than originally authorized. Other tickets simply disappeared from circulation.

"These tickets," army surgeon George Gwyther recalled a few years later, "at first made of stout card-board, were so often willfully lost, or the writing on them so skillfully forged, that stamped metal slips were substituted."[165]

Of course, the same Diné headman who knew how to write like a Bilagáana also knew how to work metal. And now he had access to a complete set of blacksmith tools courtesy of the U.S. Army. Gwyther reported that "in short time it was found that their ingenuity had enabled them to make dies and forge the impressions successfully."

So successfully, in fact, that no one could tell the difference. The soldiers didn't know they'd been conned until they counted the tin tickets they'd collected and discovered they'd taken in more than they'd handed out. After one such tally in May 1865, Captain Henry Bristol reported to the post adjutant:

In conclusion, I would state that the number of spurious tickets are increasing, and they are so handsomely executed as to be indistinguishable. Three hundred of these tickets are among the genuines and are so much alike and the same that Mr. Edgar is unable to throw them out.[166]

All told, the prisoners counterfeited more than three thousand ration tickets that year. They also successfully duplicated three hundred of Carleton's military passports, which granted anyone who slipped out of Bosque Redondo safe passage through New Mexico.[167]

The fraudulent passports may explain how Barboncito, after he was captured in Canyon de Chelly, managed to escape from Bosque Redondo in July 1865 and elude Union soldiers for more than a year. He finally returned of his own accord in November 1866, bringing with him a few families on the edge of starvation.

Similarly, Manuelito not only managed to evade capture for three years but also surreptitiously visited Bosque Redondo at least once. The most wanted man in the territory proved impossible to catch. He finally gave himself up in September 1866, after he was shot in the forearm in a skirmish with Hopi warriors and his followers lost the will to fight.

The army eventually put an end to ration ticket counterfeiting by ordering brass tokens shipped in from a federal mint, each about the size of a half dollar—impossible to duplicate under the conditions of the camp. A photograph taken at Bosque Redondo shows more than a dozen Diné men, seated on the ground, apparently under guard. It's captioned, "Navajo chiefs accused of counterfeiting ration tickets at Bosque Redondo, Fort Sumner, New Mexico." Yet there's no record of charges being filed.

Delgadito was the obvious suspect. Punishing him, however, was another matter. The general had turned Delgadito into the symbol of the supposed subjugation of the Navajo; how could Carleton admit that he'd been duped by his prisoner?

By the time the counterfeiting operation was uncovered, Carleton could not afford another scandal. His critics were growing by the month. The previous December, the *Santa Fe Weekly New Mexican* accused him of participating in the slave trade he'd forbidden. Under a headline declaring, "Carleton Gives Away One of His 'Pets,'" the paper reported:

Everybody is aware and knows that no one is allowed to have a Navajoe Indian in his possession, but I have lately learned that General Carleton

Right: One of the brass ration tokens the army made to prevent further counterfeiting, along with a silver peso favored by Diné smiths. *Author's collection.*

Below: This 1865 photo was captioned, "Navajo chiefs accused of counterfeiting ration tickets," but there's no record of charges being filed. *Palace of the Governors.*

THE COUNTERFEITERS OF BOSQUE REDONDO

presented a little Navajoe girl to a sutler, 3 or 4 months ago....I've not the slightest ill-feeling towards the sutler (who is a gentleman), but I could merely call the attention of the people of New Mexico to the fact that while many of them have been compelled to give up the Indians whom they had for many years, and who were perfectly contented with their situation, General Carleton, as a matter of economy, keeps them on hand for presents and gifts.[168]

In Washington, there were complaints about how much Bosque Redondo cost and questions about the treatment of prisoners. Carleton's superiors received reports of one deprivation after another: not enough food, not enough water, not enough firewood, children dying from dysentery and smallpox...and where was all that fabled gold?

Patience, Carleton urged. The Navajo could still thrive at Bosque Redondo. "Through all the clouds that now seem to surround this important, and, to them, vital matter, I hope soon to see some encouraging light," he wrote.[169]

Time was running out. Outcry was growing over the treatment of America's first nations, not just in New Mexico Territory but throughout the West. Newspaper reports of the Sand Creek Massacre, in which U.S. troops attacked Arapaho and Cheyenne families in their sleep, jolted readers across the country.

In March 1865, the Senate and House passed a joint resolution "directing an inquiry into the condition of the Indian tribes and their treatment by the civil and military authorities of the United States." Within weeks, army commanders in New Mexico learned that the inquiry was coming to them. Representative Lewis Ross, an Illinois Democrat, was traveling to Bosque Redondo to hold Congressional field hearings. And Herrero Delgadito, the blacksmith turned counterfeiter, would be among those called to testify.

THE CONDITION OF THE INDIAN TRIBES

Captain Henry Bristol didn't mention the counterfeiting operation. One month after finding another three hundred duplicates of the tin ration tickets, he appeared before a team of Congressional investigators at Fort Sumner and swore that the blacksmith's shop was an example of how well things were going at Bosque Redondo.

"The young men and boys seem very anxious to learn, and show much aptitude for the work," Bristol testified at the June 1865 field hearing. "They have some blacksmiths among them who make good bits; one presented, made by a Navajo, is in the Spanish style."[170]

Bristol did his best to counter the camp's growing chorus of critics. He allowed that there had been some deaths—exactly how many, he couldn't say—but he described the prisoners as a largely contented and industrious lot. "If nothing interferes to prevent the present crops from maturing, as they now promise well, I think we shall raise nearly enough to feed the Indians until next season," Bristol said.

Congressman Lewis Ross invited the prisoners to furnish witnesses of their own. The Mescalero Apache leader Cadette spoke first, telling Ross that the prisoners wanted just one thing: to go home. They had tried to make a life for themselves at the Bosque, but the people were always hungry. Dysentery, smallpox and measles claimed new victims every week. "About six days ago, four died: an old man, middle-aged man, a boy, and a girl," Cadette told Ross.[171]

The Diné chose Delgadito to speak on their behalf. He confirmed everything Cadette had said—the deprivation, the disease. By then, Delgadito had lost five of his own children.[172] A clerk wrote down Ross's questions, followed by Delgadito's answers, as translated by an interpreter:

Question: Is there plenty of wood on the reservation for fuel?

There is plenty below here, but we have to go too far for it. Don't know whether fuel could be floated down the river or not; knows of some floating down; could pack the wood if we had the burros.

The water has alkali in it, and they are afraid it will make them sick; a good many have been sick and died; when they drank the water, they took sick and died; and others have got sick by carrying mesquite so far.

Those that were attended by the doctor all died; do not know his name; he was physician at the hospital. There is a hospital here for us; but all who go in never come out. We have physicians among ourselves, but they can't cure all; some must die. They commenced to get sick about last October, and since then every day some of them have died; so many of them dying they are getting frightened; a good many of his children and grandchildren have died; three sons and two daughters have died; they are dying as though they were shooting at them with a rifle.

Question: Do the young men like to work and want to work?

Yes; the young men work well; love to work; even the women.

Question: Are your women and children all pretty well now?

All are not well; some of them are sick (all agree to what Herrero says).

Question: If your people had plenty of wool could they make all the clothes?

Yes; if we had the wool we could make all the clothes for the tribe. All of them know how to cultivate by irrigation; thinks there is plenty of land; but somehow the crops do not come out well. Last year the worms destroyed their crops.... There is plenty of pasture for all their stock; some have but 25, 30, or 40, but more have none; none have a hundred. They try and keep their sheep for their milk, and only kill them when necessary, when the rations are short or smell bad. They depend on the milk of the sheep to live and to give to the little children; they are honest and do not kill each other's sheep; they own their animals themselves, and not in common; they would like each man to have his own piece of land and work it for himself and his family; they have not grain, stock, and other things enough; when they have enough they would like to have their children go to school; they would not like to have their children go to school until they had learned all kinds of trades, so they could make a living.

Some officers at Fort Canby told them when they got here the government would give them herds of horses, sheep, and cattle, and other things they needed, but they have not received them; they had to lose a good deal of their property on account of the war, and the Utahs stole the rest from them; have been at war with the Utahs nine years, and about the same number of years with the Mexicans.

Before the war with the Utahs and Mexicans, had everything we wanted; but now have lost everything. Herrero was quite young when the war commenced with the Mexicans. In the war everything was stolen on both sides, women and children, flocks. When children were taken we kept them, sold them, or gave them back. The Mexicans got the most children;

Ordered to compile a list of slaves in his jurisdiction, U.S. Indian Agent Lafayette Head omitted those he personally held in captivity. *Fort Garland Museum.*

we have only two, and they don't want to go back; have not been in the habit of selling our own children; don't know of an instance.

They don't expect to be rich again; but if they had plenty of stock, and wagons to haul their wood, they would prosper again. Some of the soldiers do not treat us well. When at work, if we stop a little they kick us or do something else; but generally they treat us well. We do not mind if an officer punishes us, but do not like to be treated badly by the soldiers.

They say their women sometimes come to the tents outside the fort and make contracts with the soldiers to stay with them for a night, and give them five dollars or something else; but in the morning take away what they gave them and kick them off. This happens most every day. In the night, they leave the fort and go to the Indian camps; the women are not forced, but consent willingly; a good many of the women have the venereal disease. It has existed among them a good many years in their own country, but was not so common there as it is here; there are remedies to cure the disease, but they cannot get them here; they have no confidence in the medicines given them at the hospital; think it would do them no good; most of the old men know how to cure the disease; they use the root of wild weeds that do not grow here; some of the people are dying here of the disease; some were taken to the hospital, but were not cured; when they find out a person has that disease they report it to the hospital; this they have done for some time; but all they have reported there have died. The custom of the tribe is never to enter a house where a person has died, but abandon it. That is the reason they don't want to go to the hospital; they would prefer a tent out by their camps for a hospital.

By Mr. Ross to Herrero, Question: Were you made a chief by your own people or by the whites?

By my own people.

To the chiefs, Question: Would you all like to go back to your old country or remain here?

They would rather prefer to be in their own country, although they have most everything they want here; they are all of this opinion, and would like to have you send them back; and if you have any presents to give them they will distribute them among them. If they were sent back they would promise never to commit an act of hostility.

Question: If you are sent back could you make your own living?

Yes; we could support ourselves; and you could send some troops to see that we kept our promise.

Finally, Ross got to the big question, the only one the Diné really cared about:

Question. Do you want us, when we go back, to tell the Great Father and the great council that you would like to be sent back to your old country?

Yes; we would all like to go, and if sent back would go straight back the way we came.

Question: Are the soldiers treating you badly? And if so, let us know.

The soldiers about here treat us very bad—whipping and kicking us.

Question: Do you get enough to eat here?

We do not get enough to eat.

Question: How much do you get as a ration?

(No answer recorded)

Question. Is there any game in your own country?

Yes; there is plenty of rabbits, antelope, deer, and wild potatoes. Herrero says they would like to have you send them back to their own country. They think you are the greatest men and can send them back, and they would like to have it done soon.

Ross explained that he and his colleagues didn't have the authority to release anyone—they could only relay the wish to the president and Congress. Delgadito conferred with other Diné headmen and then turned to the interpreter. "They say they will try and work to do all they can to support themselves until they learn what disposition is to be made of them."

Delgadito had one other request that day. He told Ross that his name—Herrero—meant "blacksmith." He explained that he'd been training some of the other men, teaching them how to fashion bridle bits, hatchets and such. Was it possible, the counterfeiter asked the congressman, to send more tools for the blacksmith's shop?

UNBROKEN

On July 9, 1867, a skirmish broke out between prisoners and troops at Bosque Redondo. When the dust settled, a soldier had been wounded and several warriors had fled with their families.

By then, escapes were common. A few months after Cadette told Congressman Ross that all of the Mescalero Apache wanted to leave, all of the Mescalero Apache did just that. More than three hundred men, women and children disappeared one night. The soldiers never saw them again.

Carleton was gone, too, transferred out the previous fall. He petitioned a review board to let him stay, still promising that he could turn Bosque Redondo around, but the appeal was denied by the nation's top general, Ulysses S. Grant. Carleton's project on the Pecos had become an embarrassment; some called it a scandal.

Congress stopped short of closing Bosque Redondo, but sentiment in Washington had turned decidedly against it. What's more, the open secret of New Mexico's slave system had become impossible to ignore. During the course of the Congressional investigations, New Mexico Chief Justice Kirby Benedict publicly accused Governor Connelly, a fellow judge, and most of the territory's Indian Service agents of trafficking in Navajo slaves.[173]

In the spring of 1867—nearly two years after the surrender of the Confederacy and the end of Southern slavery—Congress passed an act to "abolish and forever prohibit the System of Peonage in the Territory of New Mexico and other Parts of the United States."

With so much attention on New Mexico, Carleton's replacement as the territory's commander, General George Getty, adopted a conciliatory tone toward the prisoners he'd inherited. The ration shortages had subsided by that time. Blankets, clothing—everything became easier to obtain after the Confederates surrendered.

So, when Getty learned that a fight broke out at the camp that summer, with bullets and arrows flying before cooler heads prevailed, he knew the trouble wasn't over supplies. Rather than rely on his officers' reports, he scheduled a hearing for the following month and invited twenty-two Diné headmen to attend. Flanked by three of his officers, Getty opened the proceedings and then let the Diné speak:

Getty: I told the Indians, in substance, that when I visited Fort Sumner in May last, I sent them word by Lieut. McDonald, that I was well pleased with all I had seen; that I had witnessed the issuing of food to them from the storehouses, and found that it was of good quality and issued regularly and fairly; that I had examined their fields and found the crops looking well, and promising an abundant yield; that I could see nothing to change then, but would return soon and listen to all they had to say; that I had called them together now for that purpose if they had complaints to make, I wished them to state them fully and that I wished to hear especially what they had to say about the recent troubles with the soldiers.

Delgadito: My thoughts are as they always were. My head and heart are for the right. When brought from my own country here, I was told this ground was my ground and this water my water. I intend to live here and do what is right. The first time I planted here I did not get any crop. Three times I have tried to raise crops and failed. I don't like the Bosque, because I don't think crops can be raised here. Since I have been here, I have not been able to raise even a basketful. I do not believe the ground here is the best ground for us. We have plenty of food and clothing, but can't get two of anything—if we do one disappears, we know not how. In our old country, we raised abundant crops and herds; here we can raise none. I feel sorry that we can't get sheep or cattle of any kind. It seems as if I would never see any more flocks. I have not said anything about the difficulty with the troops. I was not present, but at work; and only heard of it when I came in and found everything in confusion. I went down with Lieut. McDonald, but turned back, because I was afraid, hearing so much noise. Lieut. McDonald told me the troops were not sent down to fight the Navajos. The troops tried to drive the herd and herders along with them. A boy went round the herd and was fired at three times. The Indians thought the troops had come down to fight them and got ready for it. This is the story told me by the Indians. It was those who came last to the reservation who got into the difficulty—not knowing the laws.

Ganado Mucho: This trouble took place under the eyes of the troops, and I am glad they could see it. I want these things to be forgotten and everything to go on as before. I know that the herd was on the other side of the river and was all right. Then the troops without any notice drove the herd off. After the herd was driven off, I saw a party go down and it was from the troops that the first shot was fired. The Indian has kept silent because he knows he was not to blame, but the blame is with the troops. I feel sorry that this happened on account of the Indians who have gone off for they will suffer from hunger and thirst. I think about eight men have left—don't how many women and children. I would like to hear the General say this shall be forgotten as it shall be on our part.

Narbono: When the troops left the post, I was asleep. The noise of the horses passing by awoke me. I ran out of my house and saw the women running out of the huts crying, "The Comanches are coming!" I saw the soldiers pass and ran into the house. A woman came and told me they were fighting (the Navajos and troops). I did not wish to go down as it was like two brothers fighting. I saw the troops coming back bringing a soldier with an arrow in him. I sent a boy after my horse. I then saw Lieut. McDonald and Major Tarlton going along. My horse was not ready. As soon as he was ready, I followed and showed them where the trouble had taken place. I had no arms with me and went back for my bow and quiver, so as to be ready to help the lieutenant and the major. Manuelito caught the Lieutenant's horse by the bridle, and tried to keep him back. After I found they would not stop, I and Manuelito rode ahead. The women got on their horses ready to move off. When the Lieutenant got down there, a party came over and shook hands and wanted to talk. The Navajos told Lieut. McDonald that the troops brought on the fight. I know the troops were to blame, and had they gone down as Lieut. McDonald did, there would not have been any trouble.

Manuelito: I have not much more to say than what has been said by those before me. I thought at first that it was the Comanches making the trouble. I came out to find out if it was Comanches, as I wanted to go along with the troops after the Comanches. Some Navajos told me the troops were going after horses. I went back and met Colonel Dodd and went back to the fort. I then went after Major Tarlton who had gone out from the post. I met one Indian who told me what the matter was. I saw soon some Indians who, I thought, were going to hurt Lieut. McDonald and tried to stop him from going ahead. He would not stop, so I rode ahead. When we rode up, the Navajos came over and said they were sorry this had happened, that none of the good men of the tribe were engaged in it. We have been silent since, because we believe the blame is on the troops. We are sorry for what has happened, and have worked well ever since. We have been treated well by the officers.

Barboncito: I would like to say, that when we want to talk, we would like to meet as we do today, in a large room like this, all together. Where there is anything to be done, we would like to be told it in some place where we can all meet. We are all your family, and will [cooperate], and we don't want to be abused. I am glad to hear all you have said. We don't like the ground here. The water is not good; the corn does not grow. I used to think all land was alike. In our country we raised corn and cattle. We can't do so here. I hope you will think those are the thoughts of all the Navajos. I own nothing but my own body. I have no stock. Before I get too old, I would like to see my children in their old country as they were before. I know where we could raise plenty. We have among us the bad as well as the good. I speak the thoughts of all the Navajos. I know the Great Father is a long way off, but I am talking as if he were here. We don't believe we can raise stock here. They eat something which kills them. They die and we die. We can find no more. We want to know when we can go back to our old country.

The Diné found a sympathetic ear in Getty. In his report on the skirmish, he determined that they'd committed no wrong:

Convinced from the manner and bearing of the Indians, that they were sincere and honest in what they said—that their disposition was decidedly friendly; and that the unfortunate collision with the troops on the 9th of July was the result of a misunderstanding on their part, and had not been premeditated, I decided to convene a Board of Officers at Fort Sumner to inquire into the cause of the collision, and to defer final action in the matter, until the report of the board should be received.

    The proceedings of the board and accompanying pares are herewith submitted, and are approved.[174]

The Great Father might be a long way off, as Barboncito said, but a growing number of U.S. officials had begun to question the necessity, and even the morality, of exiling the Navajo Nation.

BEAUTY WAY

In the last days of Bosque Redondo, a song drifted out over the Pecos, rattling some of the soldiers going about their duties at Fort Sumner. Climbing onto rooftops for a better view, the soldiers witnessed something remarkable in the distance: thousands of Diné prisoners, standing in a circle so big that it ringed miles of dusty plain.

The soldiers were too far away to see the man standing at the center of the circle, much less the coyote he had with him. They would not have understood anyway. Barboncito had caught the coyote himself; the idea came from the crystal gazers.

The fate of the Diné was still uncertain then, back in May 1868. There was a chance the U.S. government would send the Navajo even farther east, perhaps all the way to Oklahoma. That's why Barboncito asked the crystal gazers to seek guidance from the holy ones.[175]

The crystal gazers did as he asked; they did not like what they learned. They told Barboncito that the proposed reservations to the east would not sustain their people. By then, more than one out of four prisoners at Bosque Redondo had already died, victims of the hunger, disease and abuse that defined the camp.

So it was agreed: After five years of exile, the Diné must return to Dinétah. Yet the U.S. government had never allowed any Indigenous nation to return to their land once relocated, not once in all the years of westward expansion. That's why the crystal gazers suggested using a coyote. A trickster by nature, the coyote had left a long trail of stories, extending back as far as First Man and First Woman. He might fool the army into changing their ways, and lead the people home.

Barboncito listened as the crystal gazers spoke. Four days later, he walked into camp with a coyote. It was bound and blindfolded in preparation for the ceremony. Barboncito began by asking the people to form a great circle around him. Hundreds turned out, then more; soon most of the camp joined in. As the circle took shape, Barboncito started to sing a prayer, and the people all joined in.

When the prayer was finished, Barboncito placed a small bead in the coyote's mouth. Made of white shell, the bead represented Changing Woman and a new beginning. Barboncito released the animal. The coyote took off, scurrying toward the east.

"Not that way!" Barboncito shouted in his own language. The people standing in that part of the circle began to shout, too, and waved their arms at the coyote. This caused the animal to turn south. It was running at full speed now. Another arc of people stood in its path, and they began to wave and shout, just as the others had. So the coyote turned again. Finally it was facing west, toward Dinétah. "Open the circle, and let him through!" Barboncito shouted.

The coyote bolted through the gap, finally clearing the great ring. It's said that the animal paused once to look back, howled and then vanished into the west, its freedom secure.

That same week, U.S. flags across the territory were lowered to half-staff, as news spread that Kit Carson had died of an aortic aneurysm at the age of fifty-eight. After the campaign against the Navajo, Carson fought the Kiowa and Comanche at the Battle of Adobe Walls. Then he moved north to Colorado, to his final home in Boggsville, on the banks of a river named Purgatoire. The river lived up to its name. Carson's wife, Josefa, died in April 1868 after giving birth to their seventh child. Already in poor health, Carson followed a month later. Lying in the surgeon's quarters at Fort Lyon, his last words were, "Adios, compadres."

General William Tecumseh Sherman considered sending the Diné farther east, until Barboncito convinced him that they should return to their own country. *Library of Congress.*

A few days later, a set of army carriages pulled into Fort Sumner carrying two men. They called themselves peace commissioners. One was a craggy-faced American general named William Tecumseh Sherman, a hero of the war against the graycoats. The other was younger, his hair still dark and thick, just a trace of crow's feet forming around the eyes. His name, Samuel Tappan, would not have sounded familiar to the Diné. They had no idea that they were looking at the one Union army commander who tried to end slavery in New Mexico as well as the South.

Sherman and Tappan invited twenty-four Diné headmen to discuss the future of the Navajo Nation, with Barboncito chosen to lead negotiations. One witness, a Swedish photographer named Valentin Wolfenstein, recorded the scene in his journal:

> *And so it started. Below an enormous canvas to protect them from the sun, they placed themselves—the peace commissioners and General Sherman, between General Getty and General Roberts. Opposite them sat Barboncito, between the interpreter and in a half-circle all around them, their sub-chiefs and the "grand jury."*[176]

Barboncito had waited years for this moment. He stood and spoke at length, praising the commissioners and assuring them that the Diné had done their best to raise crops at Bosque Redondo. He said, "We know this land does not like us. It seems whatever we do here causes death." He doubted that a reservation in Oklahoma would be any better:

> *Our grandfathers had no idea of living in any other country except our own, and I do not think it right for us to do so. Before I am sick or older I want to go and see the place where I was born. I hope to God you will not ask me to go to any other country except my own. This hope goes in at my feet and out at my mouth as I am speaking to you.*[177]

Sherman, the man who famously declared "War is hell," was visibly moved by Barboncito's words. He replied:

> *I believe you have told the truth. All people love the country where they were born and raised. We want to do what is right.*

There was a moment of celebration. Barboncito reportedly jumped to his feet as Sherman's words were translated into Diné Bizaad. He told the commissioners:

After we get back to our country it will brighten up again and the Navajos will be happy as the land. Black clouds will rise and there will be plenty of rain. Corn will grow in abundance, and everything will look happy. Today is a day that anything black or red does not look right: everything should be white or yellow representing the flower and the corn.

Barboncito was not through, however. Once again, the Americans had avoided any mention of the Diné enslaved in settlements. He did not let it pass, telling Sherman and Tappan:

I want to drop this conversation now and talk about Navajo children held as prisoners by Mexicans. Some of those present have lost a brother or a sister and I know that they are in the hands of Mexicans. I have seen some myself.

Sherman: About their children being held as peons by Mexicans, you ought to know that there is an Act of Congress against it. About four years ago we had slaves and there was a great war about it, now there are none. Congress our great council passed a law prohibiting peonage in New Mexico, so that if any Mexican holds a Navajo in peonage he is liable to be put in the penitentiary. We do not know that there are any Navajos held by Mexicans as peons, but if there are, you can apply to the judges of the Civil Court and the Land Commissioners. They are the proper persons, and they will decide whether the Navajo is to go back to his own people or remain with the Mexicans. That is a matter with which we have nothing to do. What do you say about schools, blacksmith and carpenter shops for the purpose of teaching your children?

Barboncito: We would like to have a blacksmith shop as a great number of us can work at the trade; we would like a carpenter shop, and if a school was established among us I am satisfied a great number would attend it. I like it very well. Whatever orders you leave here you may rely upon their being obeyed.

Sherman: Whatever we promise to do you can depend upon its being done.

Tappan: How many Navajos are among the Mexicans now?
Barboncito: Over half of the tribe.
Tappan: How many have returned within the five years?
Barboncito: Cannot tell.
Sherman: We will do all we can to have your children returned to you. Our government is determined that the enslavement of the Navajos shall cease and those who are guilty of holding them as peons shall be punished.

Manuelito, Barboncito and Manuelito's brother, Cayetanito, the week the treaty was signed. Barboncito's son peers over his shoulder. *National Museum of the American Indian.*

Above: Delgadito sits in the middle of treaty delegates, wearing a bandana, with a medicine bag slung over his left shoulder. *National Museum of the American Indian.*

Opposite: The Treaty of 1868, showing Delgadito's initial "X" struck through, followed by his signature. His brother Barboncito was the first to sign. *National Archives.*

> *All are free now in this country to go and come as they please. If children are held in peonage the courts will decide. You can go where any Navajos are and General Getty will give you an order or send a soldier, and if the Navajo peon wishes to go back or remain he can please himself. We will not use force, the courts must decide.*

The courts would be of little help. Settlers could simply hustle captives out of sight whenever strangers passed. For most Native slaves, freedom would come at the cost of assimilation. Baptized Catholic, young captives grew into eligible mates. They married, and their blood mixed with that of the colonizers. Their children and grandchildren blended into the communities. Their stories were told in whispers; in time, the whispers faded into rumors. Their parents and siblings were never made whole.

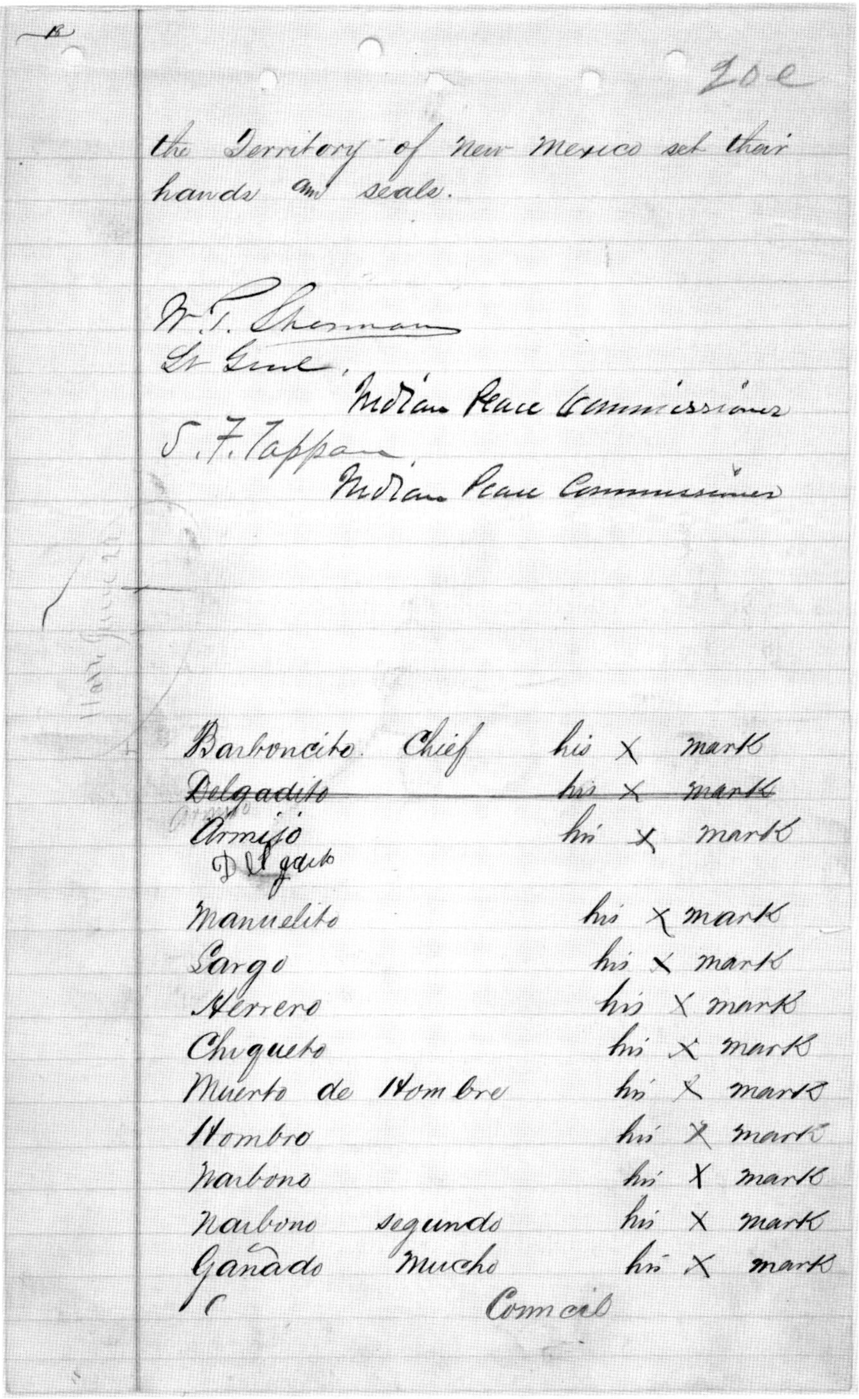

20e

the Territory of New Mexico set their
hands and seals.

W.T. Sherman
Lt Genl,
                    Indian Peace Commissioner
S.T. Tappan,
                    Indian Peace Commissioner

Barboncito. Chief   his X mark
Delgadito   his X mark
Armijo   his X mark
    Delgado
Manuelito   his X mark
Largo   his X mark
Herrero   his X mark
Chiqueto   his X mark
Muerto de Hombre   his X mark
Hombro   his X mark
Narbono   his X mark
Narbono   segundo   his X mark
Ganado   Mucho   his X mark
                    Council

Yet the seizing of Diné captives stopped that year, suddenly and decisively. If settlers were unwilling to surrender the slaves they already had, they also were unwilling to risk federal charges obtaining new ones. Baptisms of existing captives continued for a time, but just one abduction would be recorded in 1869.[178] The Diné not only secured their release from Bosque Redondo but also, finally, saw an end to the slave raids.

Barboncito, last of the great headmen to surrender, was first to put his "X" mark on the treaty. Delgadito went after him. Then came Armijo, who'd spent days searching the woods for his friend Henry Dodge back in the winter of 1856.

Manuelito was about to make his mark when someone realized that there'd been an oversight; a red line was drawn through the "X" that Delgadito had just made. Leaning over the eighth and final treaty between the United States and the Navajo Nation, he took the pen in hand again, this time signing, "Delgadito." The date was June 1, 1868.

Wolfenstein, the Swedish photographer, captured several images that week, including a group portrait of the Diné headmen. The only known photograph of Delgadito, it shows him seated on the ground, front row

Juanita in 1874, the year she participated in a diplomatic trip to Washington, D.C., along with her husband, Manuelito. *Mark Sublette Medicine Man Gallery.*

center, his hair pulled back under a bandana and a medicine bag slung over one shoulder.[179]

In another photo, Manuelito stands next to a seated Barboncito. He's wearing an impressive silver concho belt—possibly the first ever captured on film. A little boy stands just behind Barboncito, peering out over the great leader's shoulder.

A date was set for their release: June 18. When the morning finally arrived, the survivors of Bosque Redondo formed a line ten miles long. Among them walked the first generation of Diné smiths, free to turn from survival back to silver, nurturing an art form that would become recognized the world over.

Someone in the crowd began to sing. Others joined in. Everyone knew the words; it just had been a while since anyone sang them:

> *In beauty I walk*
> *With beauty before me I walk*
> *With beauty behind me I walk*
> *With beauty above me I walk*
> *With beauty around me I walk*
> *It has become beauty again*

EPILOGUE

The country carved out by the Treaty of 1868 was considerably smaller than the one Delgadito left in 1864. None of the four sacred mountains fell within its borders. Still, it was theirs. And in years to come, it would expand in every direction. Tribal leaders negotiated fourteen separate border extensions between 1868 and 1934, and Delgadito would live to see all but two of them.

Long after his hair turned white, he met a younger Diné man with a familiar-sounding name: Henry Chee Dodge. Chee was short for Kiiłchíí', or Red Boy. To this day, it's debated if he was the son of Henry Lafayette Dodge, the Navajo agent known as Red Shirt, or simply named in his honor.

Born at Fort Defiance around the time of Henry Dodge's death, young Chee was among thousands of children swept up in the Long Walk and imprisoned at Bosque Redondo. He grew up to lead the Navajo police force and serve as the first chairman of the tribal government. By the time they met, Delgadito was known by the last of his Diné names—Atsidí Sání, or "Old Pounder." Dodge recalled:

> *I knew Atsidí Sání well. He used to live over near Washington Pass, just a short way from my house. When he was an old man he used to come over here and talk with me. He was blind at that time, and I used to lead him around by a cane. He died some twenty years ago* [circa 1918], *and at that time he must have been over ninety years old. He told me that he learned how to work iron when he was a young man, I guess he must have been*

about twenty-five then. He didn't learn that up in this country. He used to go down to the south where there were Mexicans living, and it was there that he learned it from a Mexican blacksmith.[180]

Barboncito's journey was shorter. The Great Orator died just three years after securing the release of the Diné from Bosque Redondo. He was buried in his beloved canyon with one of the original copies of the Treaty of 1868—the precise location remains a family secret. In 2019, Samuel Tappan's heirs discovered another copy of the treaty among his papers and donated it to the Navajo Nation Museum. The third and last known copy is housed at the National Archives in Washington, D.C.

Alongside his wife, Juanita, Manuelito led the Navajo Nation for another quarter century. For many years, they continued to press for the return of the people enslaved in settlements. In 1872, Manuelito raised the issue again with the American general Oliver Howard. Few U.S. officials knew more about slavery than General Howard; in the immediate aftermath of the Civil War, he headed the Freedmen's Bureau, overseeing the integration of former slaves into southern society and politics. In 1867, he founded Howard University, opening the door to higher education for Black citizens on both sides of the Mason-Dixon line. Yet at a meeting with Native American leaders five years later, the general professed surprise that anyone remained in servitude in New Mexico. When Howard asked how it was that so many Navajo came to be enslaved, Manuelito scoffed:

You know very well how they came to be there. When this world was dark with dirt and sand flying, and the stones were raised by the wind, and all were fighting with the government and themselves, you know very well how this thing happened. When all the nations came against us, then we lost our children.[181]

Despite his grievances, Manuelito became a champion of the American education system. "My grandchildren," he said, "education is a ladder." He even sent two of his sons to Carlisle Indian Industrial School, which became the model for a nationwide network of residential boarding schools designed to forcibly assimilate Native children. The first step in the process was to give the children haircuts and new names, just as the Spanish priests had done. Both of Manuelito's sons fell sick their first year at the school; one died at Carlisle, and the other succumbed after returning home. Colonialism does not end—it only takes new forms.

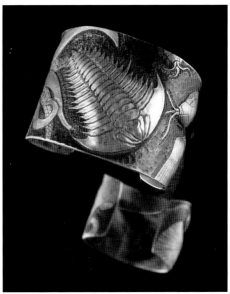

Left: Titled *The Silversmith's Daughter*, this photo was taken by J.R. Willis about forty years after the Navajo returned home. *Library of Congress.*

Right: This cuff, made in 2022 by Liz Wallace, shows how expansive Diné silverwork has become in terms of both technique and subject matter. *Liz Wallace.*

So does resistance. Washington Pass is now known as Narbona Pass, renamed in honor of the Navajo leader as a result of a campaign initiated by Diné College students in 1990. That same year, a group of Navajo Nation high school students made a four-hundred-mile trip to the state historic site at Fort Sumner. They found plenty of information about the 1881 grave of Billy the Kid, but barely a mention of the more than two thousand Diné prisoners who died while interred there. The students left a letter of protest:

> *We find the Fort Sumner Historical Site discriminating and not telling the true story behind what really happened to our ancestors in 1864–1868....*
> *We therefore declare that the museum show and tell the true history of the Navajos and the United States military.*[182]

The letter worked; the state listened. Today, that letter greets visitors to the Bosque Redondo Memorial and Museum. The museum's exhibits no longer gloss over what happened; boxes of tissues are strategically placed near the exit. Yet the memorial's emphasis is on personal strength and cultural

June 27, 1990

We the young generation of the Diné (Navajo) were here on June 27, 1990 at 7:30 pm. We find Fort Sumner's Historical site discrimminating and not telling the true story behind what really happened to our ancestors in 1864-1868.

It seems to us there is more information on "Billy the Kid" which has no significance to the years 1864-1868. We therefore declare that the museum show and tell the true history of the navajos and the United States military.

We are concern young generation of the navajos for the future.

Left: A letter that Diné high school students left at Fort Sumner Historic Site, demanding the truth be told about what happened there. *Bosque Redondo Memorial.*

Below: Designed by Diné architect David Sloan, the Bosque Redondo Memorial reflects the shapes of a hogan and a tepee. *New Mexico Department of Cultural Affairs.*

resilience. Looking back, the tragedies of those years are inseparable from the triumphs, like the warp and weft of an old wool blanket.

In 2021, the enrolled membership of the Navajo Nation surpassed that of the Cherokee Nation, making it the largest Indigenous nation in the United States.[183] The new number—399,494 men, women and children—is almost thirty times larger than the estimated population of the Navajo Nation in the 1860s. Its government maintains an office in Washington, D.C., not far from the embassies of other sovereign nations.

NOTES

Part I

1. Frank D. Reeve, "Navaho Foreign Affairs, 1795–1846: Part I, 1795–1815," *New Mexico Historical Review* 46, 2 (1971): 113.
2. Jocelyn Jean Bowden, *Private Land Claims in the Southwest* (Houston, TX: privately published, 1969).
3. Hubert Howe Bancroft, *History of Arizona and New Mexico, 1530–1888* (San Francisco, CA: History Company, 1889), footnotes.
4. Reeve, "Navaho Foreign Affairs," 113.
5. Adam Teller, Diné oral historian, canyon guide and great-great-great-grandson of Barboncito (interviews and e-mails).
6. Richard F. Van Valkenburgh, "Tsosi Tells the Story of Massacre Cave," *Desert Magazine* (February 1940).
7. Reeve, "Navaho Foreign Affairs," 114.
8. David M. Brugge, *Navajos in the Catholic Church Records of New Mexico, 1694–1875* (Window Rock, AZ: Navajo Tribe, 1968), 122.
9. David M. Brugge and J. Lee Correll, *The Story of the Navajo Treaties* (Window Rock, AZ: Navajo Tribe, 1971), 3.
10. Account drawn from two sources: Ralph Emerson Twitchell, *History of the Military Occupation of New Mexico* (Denver, CO: Smith Brooks Company, 1909), 293–95, and Charles F. Lummis, *A New Mexico David and Other Stories of the Southwest* (New York: C. Scribner's Sons, 1891), 198–200.

11. Charles F. Lummis, *Daily Alta California* 42, no. 14214 (August 5, 1888).

12. Brugge, *Navajos in the Catholic Church Records*, table, 22.

13. Lummis, *Daily Alta California*.

14. Lummis, *New Mexico David*, 198.

15. Family relationships confirmed though Adam Teller, descendant, and military correspondence—see Chacóon to Carleton, October 18, 1863, NARA, RG 393, Letters Received (C-320-1863).

16. Adam Teller, interviews and e-mail.

17. John Adair, *The Navajo and Pueblo Silversmiths* (Norman: University of Oklahoma Press, 1944), 4.

18. Lummis, *Daily Alta California*.

19. Anna Heloise Abel, *The Official Correspondence of James S. Calhoun*, introduction (Washington, D.C.: Government Printing Office, 1915), xii.

20. Medill to Calhoun, in Abel, *Official Correspondence*, 3.

21. Calhoun to Medill, in Abel, *Official Correspondence*, 33.

22. Major Patrick W. Naughton Jr., U.S. Army Reserve, *Colonel Alexander Doniphan and the 1ˢᵗ Regiment of the Missouri Mounted Volunteers in the Mexican-American War: A Historical Case Study on the Complexities of Cultures and Conflict in New Mexico* (Fort Leavenworth, KS: Command and General Staff College, 2018), 3, 122.

23. Donald Callaway, Joel Janetski and Omar C. Stewart, *Ute: Handbook of North American Indians*, vol. 11 (Washington, D.C.: Smithsonian Institution, 1986), 336, 339, 354.

24. Brugge, *Navajos in the Catholic Church Records*, 22.

25. John T. Hughes, *Doniphan's Expedition, Containing an Account of the Conquest of New Mexico; General Kearney's Overland Expedition to California; Doniphan's Campaign Against the Navajo; His Unparalleled March Upon Chihuahua and Durango; and the Operations of General Price at Santa Fe, with a Sketch of the Life of Col. Doniphan* (Cincinnati, OH: U.P. James, 1848), 71.

26. Brugge and Correll, *Story of the Navajo Treaties*, 44–45.

27. James H. Simpson, *Navajo Expedition; Journal of a Military Reconnaissance from Santa Fe, New Mexico, to the Navaho Country, Made in 1849 by Lieutenant James H. Simpson*, ed. Frank McNitt (Norman: University of Oklahoma Press, 1964), 63.

28. Calhoun to Medill, in Abel, *Official Correspondence*, 28.

29. Ibid.

30. Frank McNitt, *Navajo Wars* (Albuquerque: University of New Mexico, 1972), 145.

31. Calhoun to Medill, in Abel, *Official Correspondence*, 29.

32. Simpson, *Navajo Expedition*, 100.

33. *Condition of the Indian Tribes: Report of the Joint Special Committee, Appointed under Joint Resolution of March 3, 1865* (Washington, D.C.: Government Printing Office, 1867), A328.

34. Greiner to Calhoun, in Abel, *Official Correspondence*, 467–69.

35. Adair, *Navajo and Pueblo Silversmiths*, 4.

36. Canby to Assistant Adjutant General, December 27, 1860.

37. Adair, *Navajo and Pueblo Silversmiths*, 5.

38. Major Henry Sibley's report to Fort Defiance, November 12, 1860, NARA, RG 393, C-53-1860.

39. Adair, *Navajo and Pueblo Silversmiths*, 4.

40. Lieutenant George Campbell's report to Carleton, March 3, 1864, RG 393, Letters Received, (C-46-1864).

41. Joseph C. Ives, *The Colorado River of the West, Explored in 1857 and 1858* (Washington, D.C.: Government Printing Office, 1861), Indian Portraits Plate VII, illustrated by H.B. Möllhausen.

42. William W.H. Davis, *El Gringo: New Mexico and Her People* (New York: Harper & Bros., 1857), 411–12.

43. Samuel Wells Williams and John Robert Morrison, *A Chinese Commercial Guide, Consisting of a Collection of Details and Regulations Respecting Foreign Trade with China* (Canton: Office of the Chinese Repository, 1856), 161–62.

44. Tiana Bighorse, *Bighorse the Warrior*, ed. Noël Bennett (Tucson: University of Arizona Press, 1990), 3, 11.

45. Washington Matthews, "Navajo Silversmiths," *Second Annual Report of the Bureau of Ethnology to the Secretary of the Smithsonian Institution, 1880–1881* (Washington, D.C.: Government Printing Office, 1883), 167–78.

46. *Santa Fe Gazette*, January 7, 1854.

47. Abel, *Official Correspondence*, xiii.

48. Lawrence D. Sundberg, *Red Shirt* (Santa Fe, NM: Sunstone Press, Kindle Edition, 2013), 156.

49. Ibid., 217.

50. Ibid., 293.

51. Population estimate taken from Brugge, *Navajos in the Catholic Church Records*, 107.

52. *Santa Fe Gazette*, June 25, 1853.

53. *Santa Fe Gazette*, June 24, 1854.

54. *Santa Fe Gazette*, January 7, 1854.

55. Van Valkenburgh, field notes, and interview with Chee Dodge.

56. Raymond Friday Locke, *The Book of the Navajo* (Los Angeles, CA: Holloway House, 2002), 288.

57. Davis, *El Gringo*, 406.

58. Locke, *Book of the Navajo*, 289.

59. Davis, *El Gringo*, 407.

60. Ibid., 409.

61. Sundberg, *Red Shirt*, 422.

62. Davis, *El Gringo*, 412.

63. McNitt, *Navajo Wars*, 262.

64. The Frank McNitt Collection, National Archives, New Mexico Superintendency, T21-3, Letters, Adjutant General's Office.

65. Sundberg, *Red Shirt*, 476.

66. Brooks to Garland, July 15, 1858, Report of the Secretary of War to Congress, 35th Congress, 2nd Session, Senate Executive Document 1, 294.

67. Brooks to Collins, July 16, 1858, Records of the New Mexico Superintendency 1849–1880, Records of the Santa Fe Agency, Miscellaneous, 1857, Microfilm Reel 3.

68. Eugene C. Tidball, "John C. Tidball: Soldier-Artist of the Great Reconnaissance," *Journal of Arizona History* 37, no. 2 (1996).

69. *Condition of the Indian Tribes*, A328.

70. Ibid., A491–92.

71. Jennifer Denetdale, PhD, *The Long Walk: The Forced Navajo Exile* (New York: Chelsea House Publishers, 2007), 34.

72. Virginia Hoffman, *Navajo Biographies*, vol. 1 (Window Rock, AZ: Navajo Curriculum Center, 1978), 91.

73. Collins to Denver, September 30, 1857, Letters Received by the Office of Indian Affairs, 1824–1880, New Mexico Superintendency, Microfilm Reel 546, 1857, C1054-l674.

74. *Condition of the Indian Tribes*, A491.

75. Major Naughton, e-mail exchange, December 2021.

76. Colonel Dixon S. Miles, Order No. 4, September 8, 1855, NARA, RG 39, M-50-1858.

77. *Letter of the Secretary of State, Transmitting the Correspondence with the Governor of the Territory of New Mexico, in Relation to the Indian Disturbances in that Territory,* January 7, 1861, 36th Congress, 2nd Session.

78. *Condition of the Indian Tribes*, A334.

79. *Letter of the Secretary of State, Transmitting the Correspondence.*

80. J.H. Bill, MD, "Notes on Arrow Wounds," *American Journal of the Medical Sciences* (October 1862).

81. McNitt, *Navajo Wars*, 379.

82. William Dickinson, "Reminiscences of Fort Defiance, 1860," *Journal of the Military Service Institution of the United States* 4 (1883).

83. Ibid.

84. *Santa Fe Gazette*, September 15, 1860.

85. Brugge, *Navajos in the Catholic Church Records*, 105.

86. Major Henry Sibley's report to Fort Defiance, November 12, 1860, NARA, RG 393, C-53-1860.

87. McNitt, *Navajo Wars*, 402.

88. Ibid.

89. Brugge, *Navajos in the Catholic Church Records*, 91–92.

90. Randolph Marcy, *The Prairie Traveler*, chapter 5 (London: Trübner & Company, 1863); John Billings, *Hardtack and Coffee* (Old Saybrook, CT: Konecky & Konecky, 1887), 47–48.

91. Rafael Chácon, *Legacy of Honor*, ed. Jacqueline Dorgan Meketa (Las Cruces, NM: Yucca Tree Press, 2000), 126.

92. Diné witnesses reported that the horse's bridle had been cut.

93. *Condition of the Indian Tribes*, A313–14.

PART II

94. Aurora Hunt, *James H. Carleton: Frontier Dragoon* (Glendale, CA: Arthur H. Clark Company, 1958), 22.

95. The American garrison at Fort Sullivan included 7 officers, 80 soldiers, 4 guns and 250 militia, with inconsistent training, against a British force of 26 officers, 84 noncommissioned officers, 571 privates and 23 musicians. The British navy warships carried 116 cannons, 900 sailors and 152 Royal Marines.

96. Maine Historical Society, "The British Capture and Occupation of Eastport 1814–1818," December 2021, mainememory.net.

97. Hunt, *James H. Carleton*, 31.

98. Ibid., 85.

99. Book of Deeds, Records of Santa Fe County, 195–98, Carleton-Lane deed of trust.

100. *Rio Abajo Press*, December 2, 1863.

101. *The War of the Rebellion: Official Records of the Union and Confederate Armies*, Serial 21, Chapter XXVII, Correspondence, Union, 723.

102. John D. Young and Frank J. Dobie, *A Vaquero of the Brush Country* (Austin: University of Texas Press, 1999), 274.

103. *Santa Fe Gazette*, January 21, 1865.

104. *Condition of the Indian Tribes*, A100.

105. Julius Shaw, letter to the editor, *San Francisco, Alta California*, March 13, 1863.

106. Brugge, *Navajos in the Catholic Church Records*, 94.

107. Dee Brown, *Bury My Heart at Wounded Knee: An Indian History of the American West* (New York: Open Road Media, Kindle Edition), 22.

108. *Rio Abajo Press*, December 8, 1863.

109. *Condition of the Indian Tribes*, A114.

110. Ibid., A245.

111. Ibid., A116.

112. Jerry D. Thompson, *A Civil War History of the New Mexico Volunteers and Militia* (Albuquerque: University of New Mexico Press, 2015) 246; Lawrence Kelly, *Navajo Roundup: Selected Correspondence of Kit Carson's Campaign Against the Navajo, 1863–1865* (Boulder, CO: Pruett Publishing Company, 1970), 31.

113. Hunt Janin and Ursula Carlson, *Trails of Historic New Mexico: Routes Used by Indian, Spanish, and American Travelers through 1886* (Jefferson, NC: McFarland & Company, 2009), 136.

114. Ibid.

115. Kelly, *Navajo Roundup*, 118.

116. Ibid., 35.

117. *Condition of the Indian Tribes*, A325.

118. McNitt, *Navajo Wars*, 379.

119. Brugge, *Navajos in the Catholic Church Records*, 94.

120. *Colorado Chieftain*, June 29, 1871.

121. Kelly, *Navajo Roundup*, 6.

122. Brugge, *Navajos in the Catholic Church Records*, 96.

123. *War of the Rebellion*, Serial 41, 234.

124. Raymond E. Lindgren, "A Diary of Kit Carson's Navaho Campaign, 1863–1864," *New Mexico Historical Review* 21 (1946): 226–46.

125. Kelly, *Navajo Roundup*, 52.

126. *War of the Rebellion*, Serial 41, 728.

127. NARA, RG 393, Letters Sent, vol. 14, 213.

128. Tappan to Cooley, NARA M234, RG 75, Roll 198, transcribed by Clare "Kitty" Weaver.

129. Finnis E. Downing, "With the Ute Peace Delegation of 1863," *Colorado Magazine* 22, no. 5 (September 1945).

130. Tappan to Cutler, January 10, 1864, Colorado Historical Society, Hart Library Collection, located and transcribed by Dana R. Younger and Clare "Kitty" Weaver.

131. Order of DeForrest, March 8, 1864, Colorado Historical Society, Hart Library Collection, located and transcribed by Younger and Weaver.

132. NARA, RG 393, Letters Received (C-320-1863).

133. NARA, RG 393, Letters Sent, vol. 4, 156–57.

134. Darlis A. Miller, "Carleton's California Column: A Chapter in New Mexico's Mining History," *New Mexico Historical Review* 53, no. (1978): 1, 27.

135. Ibid., 9.

136. *Condition of the Indian Tribes*, A144.

137. Ibid., A145.

138. NARA, RG 98, Letters Received, Wardwell to Cutler, December 8, 1863, M1120, Roll 21, Frames 1,220–24.

139. Denetdale, *Long Walk*, 58.

140. *Daily Alta California*, letters to the editor, September 10, 1863.

PART III

141. Kelly, *Navajo Roundup*, 148.

142. *Condition of the Indian Tribes*, A151.

143. Kelly, *Navajo Roundup*, footnotes, 58.

144. *Condition of the Indian Tribes*, A156.

145. *Santa Fe Gazette*, February 13, 1864.

146. *Santa Fe Gazette*, February 20, 1864.

147. Ibid.

148. Campbell to Carleton, March 3, 1864, RG 393, Letters Received, (C-46-1864).

149. Brugge, *Navajos in the Catholic Church Records*, 105.

150. An estimated value of $100 in 1864 equaled more than $1,700 in 2022.

151. Kelly, *Navajo Roundup*, 119.

152. Ibid.

153. McCabe, May 12, 1864, NARA, RG 393, Letters Received, Unentered Letters Received, 1864.

154. NARA, RG 98, Letters Received, Thompson to Carleton, March 29, 1864.

155. NARA, RG 393, Letters Sent, vol. 14, 365.

156. George Gwyther, MD, "An Indian Reservation," *Overland Monthly* 10, no. 2 (February 1873).

157. Wallen to the Assistant Adjutant General at Santa Fe Headquarters, April 1, 1864, Bosque Redondo Memorial Archives.

158. Steck to Dole, January 13, 1864, NA, BIA, RG75, NMS, LR, S-234/1864.

159. NARA, Attorney General's Office, Benedict to Lincoln, July 10, 1864.

160. Knapp to Dole, February 4, 1865, Bosque Redondo Memorial Archives.

161. *Condition of the Indian Tribes*, A201.

162. *War of the Rebellion*, Serial 101, 523–29.

163. Lynda Teller Pete, *Navajo Textiles* (Boulder: University Press of Colorado, 2017), 87.

164. *War of the Rebellion*, Serial 84, 812.

165. Gwyther, "An Indian Reservation."

166. *War of the Rebellion*, Serial 102, 378.

167. Gwyther, "An Indian Reservation"; Hunt, *James H. Carleton*, 289–90.

168. *Santa Fe Weekly New Mexican*, December 9, 1864.

169. *Condition of the Indian Tribes*, A201.

170. Ibid., A344.

171. Ibid., A353–54.

172. Ibid., A354–56.

173. Ibid., A326.

174. NARA, RG 393, Microfilm 619, Roll 484, Frames 251–56.

175. Adam Teller, interviews and e-mails.

176. Valentin Wolfenstein's diary, Bosque Redondo Memorial Archives.

177. Proceedings of a Council, May 29, 1868, NA, RG 48, Treaties File, Treaty No. 372.

178. Brugge, *Navajos in the Catholic Church Records*, 102.

179. Identified by Adam and Ben Teller, descendants and Diné oral historians.

Epilogue

180. Adair, *Navajo and Pueblo Silversmiths*, 5.
181. Brugge, *Navajos in the Catholic Church Records*, 103–4.
182. Student letter of protest, June 27, 1990, Bosque Redondo Memorial.
183. Navajo Office of Vital Records and Identification.

ABOUT THE AUTHOR

Photo by Jeff Wiant.

MATT FITZSIMONS is a writer and filmmaker who lives in San Diego, California. This is his first book.

Visit us at
www.historypress.com